MOUNTAIN CLIMBER

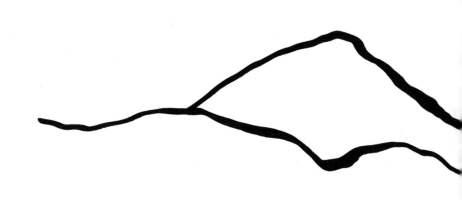

MOUNTAIN CLIMBER

George B. Bayley, 1840-1894

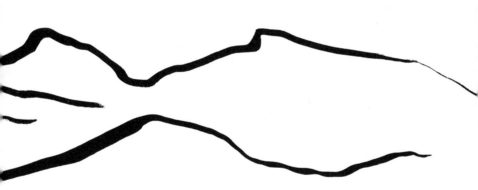

BY EVELYN HYMAN CHASE

For Janet Yelland —
In the assumption that you'd
like to know more about your
clients than their list
of assets.

Evelyn Hyman Chase

Pacific Books, Publishers
Palo Alto, California

Library of Congress Cataloging in Publication Data

Chase, Evelyn Hyman, 1912-
    Mountain climber, George B. Bayley, 1840-1894.

    Bibliography: p.
    Includes index.
    1. Bayley, George Blake, 1840-1894. 2. Mountaineers—
United States—Biography. 3. Mountaineering—
United States—History—19th century. I. Title.
GV199.92.B39C37   796.5'22'0924 [B]   80-23877
ISBN 0-87015-235-1

PACIFIC BOOKS, PUBLISHERS
P.O. Box 558, Palo Alto, California 94302, U.S.A.

To Scott and Christopher King
that they may know their great, great grandfather

Preface

FIFTEEN YEARS AGO my husband, Lionel Bayley King, knew almost nothing about his grandfather, George B. Bayley, who had died many years before Lionel was born. In 1965, Francis Farquhar's *History of the Sierra Nevada* was issued, and a copy came to our home in the California mountains for Christmas. Looking through the book that day, we found mentioned among the accomplishments of well-known Western explorers, pathfinders, and mountain climbers, four different credits to George Bayley. He was described as "one of the most remarkable mountain climbers of his time." His grandson's curiosity was aroused. Because I had been trained in historical research, we determined to look together for more detail.

A scrapbook kept by George Bayley's daughter, my husband's mother, filled with undated, unidentified newspaper clippings recounting some of Bayley's climbs, was the only bit of record we could find among Bayley's memorabilia. It gave us a start. Ten years later, after thousands of library hours; hundreds of letters to and from relatives, historians, and librarians; and thousands of travel miles, we were satisfied that we had learned all we could about this unusual California pioneer, this ancestor of the King family.

The material was ready. Since I'd had no writing experience, I enlisted the help of Barbara Young Brackett. We consulted. She worked long hours selecting and writing; she produced a manuscript that confirmed that there could be a book. *American*

West published a chapter from it.

My enthusiasm for and familiarity with what the research revealed of Bayley's exploits convinced me that the book should be focused almost entirely on the mountain climbs. I tried to rewrite the story, but found that technically I was not equipped to do so. I sought writing help from William Carter. He, too, worked long and hard producing another manuscript. In spite of his many contributions, I felt again that changes in emphasis and direction were necessary. I joined several writing classes. Backed by the support of the instructors, I gained the courage to write the book, conscious all the time of my obligations and gratitude to Barbara Young Brackett and William Carter.

My husband lived to see the research completed, to learn about his grandfather. Lionel died five years ago, believing that somehow a book would be created that would enable his many Bayley relatives, his progeny, and all outdoor-loving people to share in knowing his grandfather.

I am married again, this time into a family in which writing is a way of life. Its members share with the King family their pleasure in whatever new knowledge, new joy, new drama, and new respect for our American pioneers this book will proffer.

October 1980   EVELYN HYMAN CHASE

Contents

List of Illustrations

MOUNTAIN CLIMBER

CHAPTER ONE

The Spice of Danger

"Don't you go!" the Indian guide had begged Van Trump. The Indian's voice trembled with fear. "No one can do it and live!"[1]

For untold centuries the Yakimas had stared at the magnificent peak with feelings of awe and mystery. Their handed-down stories told of terrible gorges, bottomless crevasses, merciless gales, a fiery lake, and an infernal demon who dwelt at the summit and brooked no intruders. Towering twice as high as the surrounding Cascades, the soaring mountain was easily the most striking landmark in the Pacific Northwest. The Indians called it Takhoma; the white men later christened it Mount Rainier.

"Don't go!" the Indian guide, Sluiskin, had repeated. "You will perish if you try to climb Takhoma!"

But the white men were determined. In the summer of 1870 Philemon Beecher Van Trump, a homesteader, had daringly brushed aside Sluiskin's warnings and, with General Hazard Stevens, proved that Rainier could be scaled.[2] Within weeks, a second ascent had been made—by geologists S. F. Emmons and A. D. Wilson, who used a variation of the Van Trump-Stevens route from the west.[3] For thirteen years thereafter Takhoma's icy reaches lay unchallenged. Then Van Trump and three companions decided to attempt it again. As they gathered for this third assault, none had any way of knowing how apt the old Indian's warnings would prove.

It was July of 1883. The forty-five-year-old Van Trump, who

resided in nearby Yelm Prairie, had gained a reputation on both sides of the Cascades as an experienced farmer, miner, camper, and mountaineer. With him was James Longmire, who had crossed the plains, staked out his claim to a 640-acre section in the Yelm, and fought in the Indian wars.[4] Longmire explored the valleys and blazed the trails leading to the great mountain. In 1870 he guided Van Trump and Stevens to a spot known as Bear Prairie, where he turned them over to Sluiskin. But in all his thirty years in the valley, Longmire had never set out to climb Rainier. Now, at the age of sixty-three, he was about to try. A third man was young William C. Ewing, the son of Congressman Thomas Ewing of Ohio. Although the younger Ewing had not yet definitely decided to attempt the whole ascent, he was determined to go as high as possible and at least to witness the others' final push to the 14,410-foot summit.

The fourth man in the group was George B. Bayley, aged forty-three. He had been born in Boston, a child of New England shipping, trade, and culture on both sides of his family. At fifteen he had gone to sea. At twenty-five he had settled in San Francisco, where he became enmeshed in that youthful city's silver-lined financial world.[5] Yet his first love remained the outdoors, particularly the Sierra, and during twenty years in California he had become a highly skilled mountain climber. In an unsigned newspaper article a companion described him as:

> . . . a year or two younger than Mr. Van Trump, of small frame, well built and of great muscular development. A youthful experience of six years at sea contributed much to his natural activity, which, united to his strength, gives good grounds for a self-confidence that never leaves him in the most dangerous places.[6]

George Bayley has left his own account of this third defiance of Indian tradition, the third "impossible" assault on Rainier with no climbing tools but alpenstock, hatchet, and rope. In the September, 1886 issue of the short-lived *Overland Monthly*, Bayley was to write:

The Cascade range of mountains in Washington Territory is, without doubt, the wildest and most inaccessible region within the boundaries of the United States. Clothed with forests, whose fallen tree trunks lock together to form a continuous stockade, almost impenetrable to man or beast, furrowed by deep canyons and roaring torrents, it rises peak on peak from the valleys of the Columbia and Puget Sound to the line of perpetual snow, above which tower the culminating points of Mount Saint Helens, Mount Adams, Mount Rainier, and Mount Baker. Highest, grandest, and most inaccessible of all these is Mount Rainier, or Tacoma, the home of the only living glaciers of which the American citizen can boast, if there be left out of account a few insignificant ice fields on one of the peaks of the Sierra Nevada of California, scarcely worthy the name of glacier, when compared with the majestic ice rivers of Tacoma.[7]

He summed up his own mountaineering background with characteristic succinctness:

As a mountain climber of some experience, I had long felt the ambition to try the difficulties of Tacoma. The spice of danger is very pungent for the moment, but it leaves a delicious after-taste; and having achieved the summits of a number of western peaks, among them Mounts Whitney, Shasta, Lyell, Dana, Hood, Pike's Peak, Lassen's Butte, and, last though not least, a mountain in the Sierra Nevada named by John Muir and myself the "California Matterhorn," I had experienced in none of them except the latter such a real sample of looking destruction in the face as the Swiss climbers seem to number among their everyday experiences. If all accounts were true, Mount Tacoma could afford the only parallel on this continent to Mount Blanc, the Jungfrau, or the Matterhorn; and to it I turned with that eagerness which can best be appreciated by those who have been infected with the same sort of ambition.

And Bayley's account went on to tell what that ambition had

nurtured when he arrived in Portland, Oregon, in July of 1883:

> ... I learned by accident, and quite to my surprise, that a
> trail had been opened from Wilkeson station to the glaciers at
> the base of the mountain on the north side, and that the
> ascent to the summit could be made in one day. Wilkeson is
> the terminus of a narrow gauge railroad from Puget Sound to
> some coal mines, and thither I repaired without delay. I
> found that an excellent road had been opened through the
> forests some fifteen miles, ending abruptly at the foot of the
> grand glacier, miles in width, that pours down the northern
> face of the mountain. A glance was sufficient to demonstrate
> the impossibility of ascending the mountain on the northern
> and western sides, and that my information had been in-
> correct. I felt well repaid for the trip, however, as it brought
> me face to face with the most stupendous field of ice that my
> imagination could have conceived, and spread out before my
> eyes the whole mountain from base to summit.
>
> Retracing my route by rail to Yelm Prairie, I resumed a
> search begun a year or two before to find Mr. Van Trump,
> who had accompanied General Stevens, in his memorable
> ascent some fourteen years ago. My efforts were rewarded with
> success, and together we persuaded James Longmire, the
> hardy pioneer who had piloted the former party through the
> woods to the base of the mountain, to accompany us on an-
> other ascent. He agreed to do so if we could wait a fortnight,
> until he could gather his harvest—a condition which we
> gladly accepted.
>
> I spent the interval very pleasantly at the Canadian metrop-
> olis of Victoria, albeit with some impatience, and gladly wel-
> comed the letter that announced that the harvesting was over,
> and all was ready for the ascent.
>
> Returning at once to Yelm Prairie, we soon completed our
> arrangements. Our party was increased by the addition of a
> fourth member—Mr. W. C. Ewing, of Ohio—and on the 10th
> of August we saddled our horses, packed blankets, provisions
> and cooking utensils on the back of a faithful beast, and
> plunged into the forest.

Van Trump, who also wrote an account of the trip, credited Bayley with the leading role in its planning and direction and elaborated on the "arrangements" Bayley had made:

> Mr. Bayley superintended the organization of the expedition and laid in the supplies, and a most judicious, liberal and competent caterer did he prove. Rarely does a mountaineering party have such an outfit or regale itself on such a bill of fare as did this one. The typical mountaineer's jack-knife, plug of tobacco, flour, frying pan and coffee pot would have cut a sorry figure here. There were *(imprimis)* flour, bacon, coffee, tea (English breakfast), chocolate, canned Boston baked beans, canned codfish balls, (from Boston, too!), canned beef, potted tongue, Leibig's extract beef, jerked venison, oatmeal, potatoes, butter, sugar, condensed milk, canned apricots, canned peaches, and canned pears.[8]

However plentiful the food, the mountaineers faced obstacles and annoyances too easy to forget in our own day of insect repellent, down bags, topographical maps, and primus stoves. Yet the primary challenges were those confronted by climbers of every era: the frightening dangers of the vast, steep-walled mountain itself; the capricious hazards of the weather; and the grinding effects of fatigue, exposure, and mental stress in days and nights high above timberline. Like those before them, the four men received dire warnings of how hard it was even to reach the foot of mighty Rainier. Bayley told the story of their defiance and their success:

> The trip was regarded by all the neighborhood as foolhardy, if not absolutely impossible. We were told that there was no vestige of a trail, and it was generally predicted that we would be obliged to return before reaching the foot of the mountain. Mrs. Longmire was quite pathetic in her appeals to her husband to abandon the trip, and clung to him, saying, "Jim, you jest shaan't go." But Jim's mind was made up to go, and with true Western determination he could be deterred by nothing after the resolve was formed. Just before

starting, we were told that a party of old woodsmen, among
them Mr. Packwood, who located the old Cowlitz trail, which
we proposed to try to follow, had returned a few days before,
after one day's attempt to penetrate the forest, and reported
it impassable. With these numerous discouragements, we
were quite prepared for the five days of toil and struggle that
followed before reaching the mountain's base.

Crossing the Nisqually within an hour after leaving Yelm
Prairie, we took advantage of a fair wagon road for twenty-
five miles, gradually ascending to an altitude of eighteen
hundred feet, and terminating abruptly at Mishawl Prairie,
where we passed the night, the welcome guests of Henry, a
Klickitat Indian, who had renounced allegiance to his tribe,
adopted the dress and manners of living of the whites, married three buxom squaws, and settled down as a prosperous
farmer.

He had preempted a quarter section of land, fenced it,
erected several good log buildings, and planted his land to
wheat and vegetables, which appeared as thrifty and prosperous as any of the farms of the white settlers we had seen.
Henry was skilled in woodcraft, and we needed his services to
guide us to the mountain. For the moderate consideration of
two dollars a day, he agreed to take us by the most direct route
to the highest point that could be reached by horses, there to
remain in charge of the animals while we went forward on
foot. The negotiation was carried on in Chinook by Longmire, whose long residence among the Indians had given him
great fluency in the strange jargon, and the eloquent gestures
and contortions so essential to its interpretation. Henry knew
of the circuitous route which General Stevens had followed,
and was confident he could take us by a way thirty miles
shorter. Of this Longmire expressed doubts, but all agreed to
follow our guide until we were convinced he was in error.[9]

With these preliminaries behind them, the climbers now encountered some unexpected physical hazards:

On the following morning, the 11th, we were early in the

saddle, and trouble began almost immediately. The woods were on fire around us, and we occasionally found ourselves hemmed in by flame and blinding smoke; smouldering trunks lay across the trail, and half-burned stumps left treacherous pitfalls in our way.

Nests of yellowjackets were met with every few hundred yards, the irrevengeful inmates swarming out upon us with relentless fury. The horses were stung to frenzy, and snorted, kicked, and finally stampeded in reckless madness, until brought to a stand-still by a barrier of logs, where they crowded together, trembling with terror. Nor was this a temporary experience, but was repeated at intervals of ten minutes throughout the day. We were thus in constant danger of having our brains dashed out against the trees by the maddened beasts. The pack animals seemed to suffer most, and kicked off their packs with charming regularity about every hour.

By dint of a vigorous use of the axe in clearing the trail, we reached the Mishawl River, a distance of five miles, in four hours. The Mishawl is a clear, sparkling stream, rising in a range of mountains to the northwest of Mount Tacoma, and betraying by its purity that its birthplace was in crystal springs uncontaminated by glaciers. Four hours more of vigorous work took us six miles further, to a small brook running into the Nisqually, and by nightfall we had traversed seventeen miles from Mishawl Prairie, and gladly pitched our camp on a grassy bar of the main Nisqually.

Even in camp trials continued:

We all needed rest and refreshing sleep, but were denied either, for no sooner had we unpacked our animals than we were assailed by myriads of small black gnats and ravenous mosquitoes. The gnats were simply irresistible; one could not breathe without inhaling them; they buried themselves in one's flesh, burning like so many coals of fire; they got into every article of food, without, however, improving its flavor; they swam in the tea in such quantities that it became a nauseating *puree* of gnat, and in fact made life quite unendurable; while the mosquitoes stung and poisoned every exposed portion of our bodies. We anointed ourselves with mud, buried our heads in our blankets, and tried to snatch a little sleep, but all to no purpose. The gnats crawled down our backs, filled our hair and ears, eyes and noses; and, in short, made us so utterly wretched that not one of us closed our eyes in slumber the whole night through. This was a poor preparation for the fatigues and hardships of the following day, but we were destined to suffer the same sleepless torture for some succeeding nights before escaping to the upper region of frost and snow.

As we proceeded on our third day's journey, the forest seemed to grow denser and more entangled with fallen tree trunks, as though arranged to form a fortified stockade.

The ax was our only weapon to enable us to penetrate the barriers. Every few minutes the Indian pony in the lead would stir up a nest of yellowjackets, and away he would dash, Henry crying out at the top of his voice, "Soldiers! Hyack claterwar!" a warning to us to look out for the yellowjackets. Pushing ahead without stopping to rest, by 3 p.m. we reached Silver Creek, or Sakatash Creek, (Chinook for wild raspberry) , some fifteen miles from our last camp, and shortly after 6 p.m. made camp for the night at Copper Creek, five miles further.

What with the painful stings of the wasps, and the burning attentions of the gnats, added to the ordinary fatigues of the day, our exhaustion was complete, and we craved for sleep with an intense longing. But the gnats were, if possible, more numerous than on the previous night, and we were again disappointed.

Circumstances looked steadily worse before they looked better. The reasons for the warnings about the impossibility of reaching even the base of Rainier were rapidly becoming apparent. The endurance needed in a trackless wilderness, where climbers must also be explorers, became evident:

On the morning of the fourth day, Ewing's horse having become completely exhausted, we were obliged to turn it loose, and cache the saddle and bridle till our return. Our route still followed the foaming Nisqually, which we crossed and recrossed at frequent intervals throughout the day. At times we were forced by some impassable cliff or narrow gorge to leave the river, then we would cut our way through the forest around the obstruction, and return to the river channel, as affording fewer obstacles than the wooded mountain slopes, and greater freedom from the yellowjackets; albeit the crossings of the swift torrent were full of danger, on account of the moving mass of bowlders carried along by the stream. Between 7 a.m. and 6 p.m. we succeeded in getting fifteen miles further on our way, and made our camp for the night near an extensive series of soda and iron springs of great variety, and most agreeable to taste. Our barometer showed an altitude of 4650 feet, although we were scarcely conscious of having reached so great an elevation, as there was but little change in the character of the vegetation, or the temperature.

The black gnats never left us through the day, and were on hand in increasing numbers to partake of our supper, and cause us another miserable sleepless night. On the morning of the fifth day, a more haggard, gaunt, blear-eyed company never sat down to a breakfast of bacon and beans. In feeling and appearance we were wretchedness personified.

Just as we were about mounting for the day's journey, the pall of dense smoke that had overhung the whole country for two months lifted for a few moments, as if to revive our dejected spirits, giving us our first inspiring view of Mount Tacoma, standing out before us in clear outline, every detail distinctly marked, and bearing almost exactly northeast by compass from our position.

Our course now lay almost wholly in the rocky bed of the Nisqually River, crossing the stream with even greater frequency than the day before. Some four miles above the Soda Springs, Longmire pointed out a blaze on one of the trees, as the point where General Stevens and Van Trump had left the Nisqually for Bear Prairie in 1870. Bear Prairie lay a long

distance to the south—twenty miles at least—and was only to
be reached by crossing several high mountain ranges. To be
sure, it gave easy access to the longest of the ridges, leading
directly up to the mountain; but the way offered fresh obstacles—precipitous wooded mountains, without a trail and
without water, except at long, parching intervals. As the
mountain lay to the northeast, we were naturally averse to
turning in the opposite direction, and were all the more ready
to believe our redskin's assurance that we could continue
directly up the Nisqually. To his guidance we therefore en-
trusted ourselves confidently, and at 11 a.m. had the satisfaction of arriving at the foot of the great Nisqually glacier, an
abrupt wall of ice five hundred feet high, filling the whole
valley from side to side. Here the river, born to maturity,
springs like the Rhone from a dark blue cave in the ice. Our
barometer marked altitude at this point of 5850 feet.

The last few miles of the ascent were exceedingly difficult
and dangerous. The river bed was inclined at an angle of
about twenty degrees, and the ice-cold water reached to the
bellies of the horses. Several times our pack animals were in
imminent danger of losing their footing, and rolling over and
over. The narrow gorge echoed with the roaring, rushing
sound of the waters, and the clicking of the bowlders bump-
ing against each other as they rolled down the stream. The
water, soon as it left the glacier, was white with sand, ground
up from the granite by the resistless forces constantly at work
under the ice-river—a characteristic of all streams of glacial
origin.

Crossing the stream to the south side for the last time, we
unluckily pitched our tents over a nest of hornets—and not
until the ponies had kicked themselves free of packs and other
encumbrances, could we manage to secure them, and check
an incipient stampede. The horses were by no means the only
sufferers from this last vicious attack, as we were all badly
stung, and carried the pain in swollen faces for the rest of
the day.

On either side of the river, the sides of the ancient glacial
moraines were precipitous for more than one thousand feet in

height; the glacier in front of us was a wall; and it seemed at first sight that we had got into a box, from which the only way out was by the route we had come. Van Trump thought we should have gone by the old route by Bear Prairie; Longmire was dubious of the outcome; but Henry was perfectly

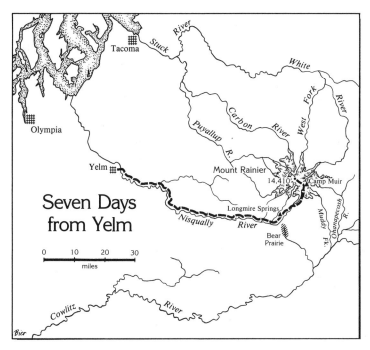

Map showing the route taken by the George B. Bayley party on its seven-day climb from Yelm to the summit of Mount Rainier in 1883. (Map by James A. Bier)

serene, and shouldering the ax, proposed cutting a zigzag trail up the mountain, as he assured us most earnestly that he could take the horses to the top of the moraine.

Even Bayley's reportage of such trying and exhausting circumstances was laced with his feelings for the beauty of the landscape:

While the remainder of the party were engineering the trail, I started a fire, and got the dinner under way, and eagerly ran down to examine the glacier. Its face was not so abrupt a wall as it had appeared, and I found I could climb to the top of it without difficulty. Its width was about two hundred feet, and its height over four hundred feet, confined between polished walls of grayish white granite. The river welled up from the dark blue cave at its foot, milky white, and heavily charged with fine sand. At frequent intervals quantities of large bowlders were hurled out, and went rolling down the steep canyon with a deafening noise like the roar of artillery. It was a most fascinating scene, and I left it with reluctance to return to my neglected culinary operations. The party had finished a trail in my absence, returned to camp, and finished the preparation of lunch.

Resaddling our animals, we succeeded in driving them up the trail with the greatest difficulty, and reached the top of the moraine after an hour and a half of toil and struggle. Continuing to ascend, we changed our course to due east, and in an hour emerged upon a beautiful plateau of gently rolling ground, where there was unfolded to our delighted eyes a superb panoramic view of Tacoma and all its southern and eastern approaches. The canyon of the Cowlitz, with its great glacier, lay to our right; the Nisqually glacier with its many tributaries to our left, and before us the long, sinuous, ragged ridge by which we knew lay our only hope of ascent. We were really only at the foot of the mountain, and thanks to Henry's sagacity had reached exactly the proper point, by the most direct and easiest possible route. Van Trump recognized his position and the route of approach which he and Stevens had followed from Bear Prairie, and realized the great distance that we saved.

The more Alpine the scenery, the more exuberant Bayley became. His observations were those of an experienced naturalist—precise and inclusive.

Our way now led us through rich grassy meadows, with

snowbanks jutting into them like headlands in an emerald ocean, fragrant flowers, of loveliest hue, were growing right up to the edges of the snow, and the whole scene was one of enchantment.

Across this meadow we rode for four miles, now floundering in snow, and at the next step rioting in a wilderness of flowers, coming finally to a steep, icy acclivity; ascending which, we came upon the last vestige of timber, a few stunted, gnarled, and storm-beaten balsam firs. A few steps away lay a little gem of a meadow, some fifty feet in diameter, almost surrounded by snow, with a pretty little rivulet of ice cold water trickling through it. The meadow was thickly strewn with large blue gentians, red castilleia, yellow polygonum, white erigeron daisy, white alpine phlox, yellow and white fritillaria, yellow armea, and a large, blue, composite flower, all of the most brilliant coloring imaginable. Here we made our final camp with our horses, and turned them loose to graze—although it seemed almost a sacrilege to see them trample and eat the dainty, gorgeously colored flowers. Our altitude here was 8200 feet, but none of us yet experienced any discomfort from the rarity of the air, or the chilliness of the atmosphere. The night was a grand one, compensating us for all the discomforts we had suffered in the lower regions. The moon shone full and clear, revealing all the landscape above and below us with startling distinctness. The long ridges of the mountains, running away to the south like a silver thread in its narrow gorge, until lost in the heavy bank of smoke that had settled down some thousands of feet below us; while overtopping and overshadowing all rose the vast bulk of Mount Tacoma, glittering coldly in the moonlight.

No insects here disturbed our rest, and for the first time in several nights we slept soundly, not leaving our blankets until eight o'clock next morning, when we prepared for climbing in earnest. The saddle animals were turned loose, and the pack horses were lightly loaded with a pair of blankets for each man, provisions for two days, and a small bundle of firewood. We started at nine o'clock, bidding adieu to the last vestige of vegetation, and after ascending over four miles of

snow, at times with great difficulty, at last came to a point the
steepness of which forbade further progress with horses. We
then unpacked them, and gave them into charge of the Indian, whom we instructed to kill some of the mountain sheep
that we had seen before leaving camp.

Henry, who had not spoken a word the entire day, and had
looked as blue as possible, here made a last persuasive appeal
to Longmire not to persist in his foolish attempt to scale the
mountain. For the rest of us he did not seem to care, but on
Longmire, as an old friend and neighbor, he wasted quite an
amount of Chinook eloquence, to save him from what he
considered certain death. He said we should never get back
alive, if we succeeded in reaching the top; while if we were
permitted to go part way by the spirit who dwelt at the summit, we should return maimed for life. He doubtless felt as
he spoke, and parted from us in a most dejected frame of
mind, as he turned to go back with the horses.

Shouldering our packs, which were apportioned to give
about twenty-five pounds to each, we traveled in an easterly
direction over the snow for about three miles, when we came
to a narrow ridge of burnt and blackened rock, running north
and south. All about us, to the right and to the left, were vast
and terrible defiles, and before us, connected with the rock on
which we stood by a steep and narrow neck, lay the last thin
backbone of columnar basalt, leading directly to the summit
dome of the leviathan of mountains. Beyond this point it was
impossible to find a spot sufficiently level to lie down and
pass the night, and as it was late in the afternoon we prepared to camp.

Van Trump reported that he had wanted to go on, but that
Bayley's judgment prevailed.[10] Bayley mentioned only that they
made camp midst the wondrous sights and sounds of the moon-
lit night:

> We lighted a fire with the few sticks of wood we brought,
> and prepared a place to sleep by throwing out the rocks, and
> making holes large enough for each to lie in. Our altitude

here was about 11,300 feet; the wind was blowing strongly from the north-west; and the thermometer at sundown marked 34. We felt this sudden change of temperature keenly on account of the wind, and gladly wrapped ourselves in our blankets.

The brilliant moonlight and the singularly clear atmosphere rendered all surrounding objects as distinct as in daylight. The sea of smoke and vapor lay six thousand feet beneath us, and as we gazed out upon its white, level expanse, so calm and limitless, it required no effort of the imagination to fancy we were on an island in mid-ocean. Mounts Saint Helens, Adams, and Hood appeared like conical islands of crystal, serene and solitary, rising from the sea far to the south of us. At times, a puff of wind would set the vapor in motion, tearing it in tatters, and rolling it up like a scroll, unveiling for a few moments the great valleys, and the vast expanse of forests, far below; and the fog would roll back again, filling up the gaps evenly, as before.

Lying due west of us, some three miles away in an air line, was the largest glacier any of us had seen, with a length which we estimated at five miles, and a perpendicular depth of probably fifteen hundred feet. It was torn and rent with enormous fissures, the blue color of which we could clearly distinguish in the moonlight, even at so great a distance. The surface of the glacier was strewn with detached blocks of masses of ice, that appeared to have been upheaved and thrown out by some mighty power struggling underneath to escape. Some of these cubical blocks must have measured hundreds of feet in every dimension, and could be distinguished twenty miles away.

The noises all night from the grinding of the glaciers was terrific. Avalanches of snow and ice from the sides of the gorges fell with a sullen crash, and every puff of wind brought showers of stones from the tops of the crumbling cliffs to the glacier; while above all other sounds could be heard the deep boom of the bowlders rushing along the rock-bound channel underneath the glacier. The mountain seemed to be cracking and groaning, and one could almost fancy that at times it gave a mighty shudder, as if to free itself from its icy shackles.

No pen can picture the fascination of these weird sights and sounds. It was only after many hours that tired nature asserted herself, and closed the senses in sleep.

NOTES

1. Aubrey L. Haines, *Mountain Fever, Historic Conquests of Rainier* (Portland, Ore.: Oregon Historical Society, 1962), pp. 42, 43.

2. P. B. Van Trump, "Mount Rainier," in *Mazama*, II (October, 1900), pp. 1–18.

3. Hazard Stevens, "The Ascent of Takhoma," in *Atlantic Monthly*, XXXVIII (November, 1876), pp. 511–33.

4. Haines, *Mountain Fever*, p. 19.

5. *San Francisco Directory, 1862.*

6. "Mount Tacoma," *The Daily Oregonian* (October 1, 1883).

7. George B. Bayley, "Mount Takhoma," *Overland Monthly*, VIII (September, 1886), pp. 266–78.

8. P. B. Van Trump, "Ascent of Mount Rainier," *Transcript* (Olympia, Washington Territory, September 8, 1883).

9. Bayley, "Mount Takhoma."

10. Van Trump, "Ascent of Mount Rainier."

CHAPTER TWO

A Delicious Aftertaste

THE FOREBODINGS OF Indian Henry, uttered when the men left him, had sounded much like those of his predecessor, Sluiskin: the four white men faced certain death if they persisted in trying to reach the top of awesome Takhoma. Yet Henry's warnings, like Sluiskin's, had been ignored. The Chinook had been sent back with the horses. The climbers had labored up the blindingly bright snowfields under the weight of their backpacks and had spent the night huddled against the freezing winds above the timberline. Bayley described what they faced when they awakened on the seventh day out, August 16, 1883:

> ... As we opened our eyes, the prospect was forbidding. It was snowing and hailing briskly, and the mountaintop was hidden in fog. The wind had changed to the southwest, and all indications pointed to an imminent storm. Before we had time, however, to regret our ill-fortune, the wind shifted to the north-west, and we were treated to a clear, beautiful sunrise, and an unobstructed view of the mountain to its summit. Springing from our blankets, we soon had a fire started, breakfast prepared, and by five o'clock we were ready for the final ascent.[1]

The men were apprehensive as they made careful preparations for the assault on the summit:

We hoped to be able to reach the summit and return to

our lofty camp by nightfall; but still we feared the worst, and
made what little preparation we could toward passing the
night on the summit. It was out of the question to think of
burdening ourselves with blankets, as they too much im-
peded our climbing, but we took a little food with us. Un-
fortunately, a bottle of alcohol, with which we expected to
be able to make hot tea or soup on the summit, though carried by Van Trump with the greatest care, was broken at our
last horse camp; and when that accident occurred, I threw
aside as useless the spirit lamp, a tin cup, and a jar of Leibig's
meat extract—not thinking of the possibility of our finding a
natural steam-heating apparatus and only having in view the
necessity of lightening our load. Besides, we were certain that
with so early a start from so high an altitude, we should be
able to return to camp again that night. I carried one hundred
feet of new manila rope; Van Trump, a hatchet and a six foot
flag-staff, hewn from a dead fir; Longmire, the whisky flask;
and Mr. Ewing brought up the rear with the barometer.[2]

The difficulties, tensions, and risks quickly became apparent:

Starting off briskly across some three hundred yards of
hard snow, we were soon climbing a black ridge of loose rock,
standing at an angle of forty degrees, and requiring most dex-
trous and active use of hands and feet. Two hundred feet of
this sort of climbing inspired Mr. Ewing with the discovery
that he preferred to return to camp and watch our attempt, so
the barometer was transferred to Van Trump, and we left
him [Ewing] behind.

Ascending a few hundred feet further over the crumbling
rocks, which were loosened by every step, we found ourselves
forced by the increasing steepness of the ridge and the volleys
of stones at short range, to the edge of the glacier. This was
no better. The ice lay at a frightful angle—a single misstep
would have hurled us thousands of feet. We were three hours
cutting some two hundred steps in the ice, a task of which we
relieved each other at frequent intervals. At the end of that
time we were again able to take to the rocky ridge, and held

to it for over an hour, when we were forced to resume our ice-chopping at the edge of the glacier, and for some time we alternated between ice steps and steep and dangerous scrambling over the loosened rocks on the side of the adjacent ridge.

Ten o'clock brought us to the top of the highest ridge, and to a view of the point of its junction with the vast *mer de glace* that swept downward in an unbroken sheet from the summit of the mountain. Looking downward from here, the great Nisqually glacier appeared to be flowing directly below us, in a due southeast direction. The debris from the ridge on which we stood went down to meet it at an angle of nearly sixty degrees, occasionally breaking off in a sheer precipice, as the walls were exposed. The view in every direction was one of solitary grandeur.

Despite the rigors and dangers, Bayley's unflagging appreciation for the esthetic continued. Then new uncertainties appeared, and hard decisions showed the correctness of his judgment and underscored the fact that he was the expedition leader:

A halt was here called, and a consultation took place as to the route by which we should proceed. Van Trump could scarcely recognize his surroundings, on account of the great changes that had taken place in the face of the landscape since his first ascent, but was under the impression that we must descend, and get upon the edge of the glacier upon its western side. I was not in favor of this, feeling confident it was practicable for us to follow the ridge, and from its terminus reach the head of the glacier. We determined to proceed as we were going. Climbing over alternate ice and rocks, we finally came to a point where the ridge diminishes to a thin, crumbling knife edge, running squarely against a huge, perpendicular precipice of rock, rising grandly one thousand feet above our heads, and standing sharply out from the main bulk of the mountain, a mighty landmark, distinguishable for many miles in every direction.

Unless we could succeed in crawling around the face of
this precipice, all further progress was at an end, as there
were nothing but yawning chasms below us on either side of
the knife ridge, reaching down hundreds of feet to glaciers
on both sides; and to have scaled the face of the wall in front
of us would have been useless as it was impossible, for we
should have been on an isolated rock, from which we should
have to descend again to proceed on our way. To add to our
discomfiture, while we were deliberating, an avalanche of
stones and dirt came over the cliff from its top, covering the
head of the glacier, and loosening from the foot of the cliff
tons of debris, which went booming down the icy slopes with
a sound like the roar of thunder.

Feeling responsible for having brought the party into this
perilous situation against Van Trump's inclination, I ran
ahead as fast as I could, crawling on all fours over the dizzy
knife edge, till I came squarely up against the cliff, where to
my great joy, I found a narrow ledge some four feet wide, on
the face of the cliff, apparently leading around to the head of
the Nisqually glacier. I shouted for my companions to follow,
as the way was clear, and without waiting for them, crept on
along the ledge some two hundred feet, where I found progress barred by an immense icicle, which had formed from
dripping water from the top of the cliff. When the others
came up with the hatchet, we soon cut a hole through the
icicle, and in ten minutes more of sharp work, clinging in mid
air to the side of the cliff with fingers and toes, and painfully
crawling past critical points of danger, we were at the head of
the glacier, which here became a steep gutter of green ice.

Luck had been on Bayley's side; insurmountable obstacles
had been overcome; and now the wild mountainside confronted
Bayley and Van Trump with its toughest challenges:

We had barely congratulated ourselves upon having safely
run the gauntlet, when another furious shower of stones came
over the cliff, falling but a few feet behind us, while a few
came directly down the ice gutter, warning us that the sooner

we were out of that locality, the better would be our chances for preserving whole limbs. There was no way for it but to follow up the gutter of ice; and for three quarters of an hour we experienced the severest and most perilous work of the ascent. Let the reader imagine the shady side of the steepest gothic roof he has ever seen, covered with hard, slippery ice, unsoftened by the sun, and prolonged for hundreds of feet above, and thousands of feet below, and he will have a fair idea of the situation. Every step had to be carefully selected and well chopped out of the ice. The consequences of a slip here may be readily imagined; it meant a swift slide of a thousand feet or more into the yawning jaws of a beautiful green and blue crevasse, which we had admired from the

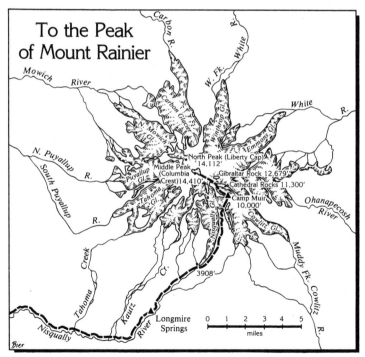

Map showing the route of the ascent to the summit of Mount Rainier in 1883. (Map by James A. Bier)

knife-edge ridge.

Laboriously and slowly carving our way up the gutter at
twelve o'clock we reached the broad stretch of billowy snow
that swept unbroken to the summit, apparently within easy
reach. For hours we had been looking forward to this snowfield, with pleasant anticipation of rest and relief from hard
climbing. We expected to make rapid headway, and reckoned
on skipping along to the summit in a few moments; but on
the contrary, we found it about the most fatiguing part of the
day's work. The snow was frozen into ice-waves, running
across the face of the mountain, and resembled a heavy chop
sea, solidified and set up at a considerable angle—the hollows
being three feet deep, hard and slippery, and the crests so
softened by the sun as to make sure footing impossible. Every
few moments we would fall down into the hollows, thoroughly spent and exhausted, or by a misstep would find ourselves forcibly seated astride the ridges. After a time we tried
a new method. The man in the lead would leap upon the
crest of the snow ridge, and pack the snow with his feet before
the others followed, and in this way we made better progress.
Every few minutes the rear man would take his turn in the
lead, and by a short period of extra exertion prepared the
little platforms on the snow crests to give sure footing for the
others to follow. Taking frequent pauses for rest, we finally
surmounted this wearisome portion of our journey, and at
three o'clock p.m. we stood upon the bare rim of the eastern
crater of the middle summit, with the upper edge of the
crater only a few hundred yards away, and about one hundred feet higher.

Thus far on our ascent, the mountain had sheltered us
from a furious gale of wind blowing from the north, which
here assailed us with such force that with the greatest difficulty we accomplished the remainder of the distance, and at
3:30 p.m. planted our flag on the topmost crest, in the face of
the bitterly cold blast.

Van Trump added interesting detail to the story of the plant-
ing of the flag:

There is a vast dome-like mass of snow near where the
crater rims touch, which was found to rise considerably
higher than the rocky summit of the mountain. In the center
of the top of this dome of snow the three companions, taking
turns at the bleak task, drilled, or punched, with alpenstocks a deep hole, in which they firmly fixed the flagstaff.
The flag is a bright red one, two feet wide and six feet long,
and if the winds do not wear it out before the smoke and
mist that obscure the mountain clear away, it is hoped that it
may be seen from the Sound through the medium of a powerful glass.[2]

Less interested than Van Trump in advertising their feat to
distant onlookers, Bayley's eyes roamed elsewhere, to faraway,
changing pictures:

The view was inexpressibly grand and comprehensive,
although the whole landscape, below an altitude of five thousand feet, was swallowed up in a sea of vapor, leaving the
higher mountains standing out like islands, as we had seen
them the night before. An occasional gust of wind would tear
open the veil for a few moments, exposing to momentary view
the precipitous canyons and crags for thousands of feet down
the mountain's sides. We seemed to be floating in a dark
blue ocean, having no connection with the earth below, and
the mountain appeared to rest gently upon its encompassing
clouds.

The narrow ridge upon which we stood was the dividing
line between two craters, nearly circular, opening out to the
east and to the west, their rims inclining from each other at
an angle of about fifteen degrees. The western crater, the
larger of the two, was some four hundred yards in diameter,
and filled with snow up to within sixty feet of its rocky edges.
Occasional small jets of steam, issuing from the base of its
rugged walls, gave evidence of former volcanic activity. We
could look down into the other and slightly smaller crater,
also, whose rocky walls, like those of its neighbor, stood out
bare and distinct above the snow throughout their entire

periphery. Jets of steam were rising from this one also at
various places.[3]

Having taken stock of the view with the rapture of a poet and
the specificity of a geologist, Bayley turned his attention to mat-
ters of immediate import. Time and nature combined to make
an unwelcome decision for the three climbers:

> By the time we had explored both craters, another hour
> had passed, and all thought of descending the mountain that
> night had to be abandoned. Indeed, had we turned back the
> moment we reached the top, it would have been impossible,
> before the darkness overtook us, to pass under the perilous
> cliff, where even now we could see showers of stones flying
> down to the glacier below; and the attempt must have proven
> fatal. The only thing that could be done was to seek some
> sheltered nook, and pass the night as best we could.
>
> To pass the time till dark, a suggestion was made to scale
> the north peak of the mountain, about a mile away; but the
> steadily increasing wind admonished us that we had better
> not run the risk of being blown over the narrow ridge by
> which lay our only path to the peak.

So they abandoned their try for the north peak. Failure of its
conquest continued to haunt Bayley until he could make a
second try nine years later. Now the men faced other challenges:

> After a long search, Van Trump finally found the ice-cave
> where General Stevens and himself had found shelter for the
> night in 1870; but alas! the roof had melted away, leaving
> only a circular well in the ice some six or eight feet in depth,
> and about eighteen feet in diameter. From a small and irregu-
> lar hole in the center issued a scalding jet of steam about the
> size of one's little finger, around which still remained the
> loose rocks piled up by the last tenants of this rude hostelry.
>
> Rebuilding the low wall to enclose a space large enough
> for their bodies to lie in, Longmire and Van Trump stowed
> themselves away inside the wall and on either side of the

steam jet; while with hatchet and alpenstock I leveled off the stones for a short path, some seven feet long, inside the cave, and prepared to pass the night pacing to and fro to keep from freezing, preferring this weary exercise to scalding myself with the steam, which had already saturated the clothing of my companions. It was a dreary outlook for the night, as the thermometer soon fell to twenty degrees Fahrenheit, and the wind howled, and roared, and poured down into our ice-walled cave, upon our unprotected heads, with a fury that made us long for the warm blankets we left in camp. I succeeded in keeping tolerably comfortable till midnight on my feet; but finally, overcome by drowsiness, and after repeated falls and bruises on the sharp rocks, was obliged to join my comrades around the "register."

Van Trump, too, gave a graphic account of the effects of the altitude and elements upon the men:

The rapidly increasing cold and the peculiar and the sickening odor of the steam were already producing their effect on the unfortunates. Their limbs were becoming numbed, their appetites had vanished (notwithstanding the long day's toil) and the thoughts of supper were repugnant, and their minds were growing dull and lethargic. Longmire and the writer threw themselves down on the stones near the steaming orifice and let the cloud of steam (its scalding heat tempered by passing through the frosty air) envelope their persons. In less than two hours they were wet to the skin, their clothes reeking with warm moisture, and whenever during the night a fierce gust of wind would sweep down from above they would shiver in the freezing blast. Sometimes a sudden puff of steam would pass over their faces and it seemed as though the skin were being scalded off. . . .[4]

Bayley blistered the ends of his fingers drawing stones out of the steaming hole in order to warm his feet. Yet he also retained enough clarity of mind to savor that "delicious after-taste" he was experiencing even before the dangers were over:

Notwithstanding the discomfort and misery of our situation, one could not but take note of the weird beauty of the
night, and the brilliant prismatic effects of the full moon,
directly over our heads, shining from a cloudless sky upon the
ice-walls of our cavern. Not even the ice-palace of Montreal,
illuminated with myriads of electric lights, could rival in
beauty the wonderful colors displayed in our fairy grotto by
moonlight.[5]

Bayley's fairy-grotto impressions were soon dispelled by the
sobering realities of daybreak:

The long night at last wore away, and by morning we were
fairly cooked by the steam. We could face it but a few moments at a time, and when we turned around, our clothing
was instantly frozen to sheets of ice.

At six the next morning, August 17th, we shivered about
the steam jet, and discussed plans for the descent. The thermometer indicated sixteen degrees, and the wind was blowing
at the rate of one hundred miles an hour, and shifting to the
southwest, with strong indications of snow. . . .

Dreading a storm, we decided not to wait for the wind to
subside, and at 7 a.m. left our friendly steam jet and started
our descent. Scarcely were we outside the cavern before our
clothing was frozen solid, and we were hurled with great vio-
lence upon our faces. Staggering and crawling along upon our
hands and feet, we managed to reach the western rim of the
large crater, where we found a partial shelter from the force
of the gale behind some large rocks, which allowed us to take
our breath—but so benumbed with cold as to be scarcely able
to grasp our alpenstocks. We discussed the route by which
we should return to the east slope of the mountain. One
favored crossing the large crater and scaling its opposite wall,
but the terrible wind raked it fore and aft, and we must have
perished in the attempt.

Once again Bayley made the decision and led the way:

While the others hesitated, I set the example, and gathering all my strength, started at my best speed along the rim of the crater.

I had not gone one hundred feet before I fell among the rocks, completely exhausted and benumbed. The others followed. Longmire also fell heavily, receiving severe cuts and bruises before reaching me. We continued crawling along slowly and painfully, a few feet at a time, all the while clinging to the rocks for dear life, to prevent being blown away by the gale, until at 9 a.m. we got around sufficiently under the lee of the mountain to be out of the wind, and reached the billowy snowfield that had so wearied and vexed us on the ascent.

Following our trail of the day before, we sprang from crest to crest with accelerating pace, momentarily cheered by the fast increasing warmth of the sun. Ten o'clock brought us to the ice gutter at the head of the glacier, where we used the rope to good advantage. Two of us were lowered the rope's length at a time, while the last man lowered himself by doubling the rope over projecting knobs of ice, and so getting down half the rope's length at a time. The high cliff was passed safely, although volleys of rocks fell on our path immediately after we had gone by.

Twelve o'clock found us half way down the burnt ridge, and within half an hour of camp, when we missed the trail, and wandered over a labyrinth of crumbling rocks for two hours, before we reached our bivouac, where we found Ewing, who was becoming very uneasy at our protracted absence. His little fire of two sticks served to give us a cup of hot tea, which, together with bread and butter, we devoured with the appetites of famished wolves, as we had eaten nothing in the two days of our absence. Food seemed so distasteful on the mountain-top, doubtless owing to our exhausted condition, that, though abundantly provided, we were unable to masticate it.

They resumed their descent at three o'clock that afternoon. Almost immediately the four of them were enveloped by a fog so dense that Bayley, who was in the lead, could scarcely be discerned by whoever was bringing up the rear. Nevertheless, by letting out periodic war whoops, he was able to keep the men in a line; and at five p.m. the weary adventurers reached the spot where they had left Indian Henry to wait for them. Bayley described what they found:

> An unbroken stillness and solitude reigned in camp. Neither Henry nor the horses could be seen or heard. The tent was found more carefully stretched than when the party left it, a trench had been dug about it, the provisions and camp equipage had been piled and covered in the center of the tent, and at either end a scarecrow, or rather scarewolf, had been improvised—the large fresh tracks of a wolf had been noticed on the snow not far from camp. All these preparations indicated that the Indian had made a movement not on the programme of the white man. Later in the evening, after much whooping and several revolver shots by one of the party, who had gone some distance down the slope, Henry made his appearance, and proceeded to explain—with a preliminary ejaculation of his relief from a grave responsibility. He had concluded that the party had been lost on the mountain, and he had put their house (tent) in order, removed the horses to good pasturage below, had moved his "ictas" (personal effects) to that point, provided himself with a few days' rations, and on the morrow had intended to start for home, to relate to their friends the supposed tragic fate of the mountaineers. It had been sad and mournful business for him, but his joy at our return was as genuine as his surprise, and we doubted if he really believed that we had reached the top at all.

That night Indian Henry may have doubted, but he had a *closh tumtum*—a happy heart. Now there remained only the wearisome, insect-infested trek back to Yelm:

> The next morning, August 18th, there came a flurry of snow that inclined us to lie abed, and it was not till nine

o'clock that we were once more under way, in full force, with blankets and all our effects packed on our horses. We adhered to the route by which we had come, and during the four succeeding days of travel encountered but a repetition of the experiences already described; a renewal of the plague of gnats and mosquitoes by night, with a running accompaniment of yellowjackets by day.

Four days later the exhausted party reached their starting point. Though bruised, blistered, and bitten, George Bayley was again in the throes of that "delicious after-taste":

The achievement was a great satisfaction to all of us—to Van Trump, because it vindicated his former claims to the distinction, upon which doubts had been cast in the neighborhood; to Longmire, because it gave him renewed pride in his manly vigor which sixty winters of hardship had in no wise undermined; and to the writer, because he realized that all other mountain climbing in which he had indulged was a boy's play compared to the ascent of this—the king of all the mountains of the United States.

Among the three who reached the top only Van Trump had previously scaled the mountain. But this time the leader was Bayley. He made the critical decisions: where to camp on the ascent, which way to go along the *mer de glace,* several methods of getting past ice barriers, the final decision not to try the north peak, the crucial decision as to how to descend, and even the decision to whoop that brought the men through the fog.

The abandonment of their intent to climb the north peak, the only exception to the complete success of the expedition, was to nag Bayley for nine years, until he returned to Mount Rainier to explore the still untrodden north crater and north peak. The ascent yet to come would prove to be the most harrowing adventure of his entire career—one that would very nearly cost him his life.

NOTES

1. George B. Bayley, "Mount Takhoma," *Overland Monthly,* VIII (September, 1886) , pp. 266–278.

2. P. B. Van Trump, "Ascent of Mount Rainier," *Transcript* (Olympia, Washington Territory, September 8, 1883) .

3. Bayley, "Mount Takhoma."

4. Van Trump, "Ascent of Mount Rainier."

5. Bayley, "Mount Takhoma."

CHAPTER THREE

The First Two Hundred Years

BY THE TIME George Bayley was twenty-two and had come from the East to the West,[1] he was staking out a claim to a future in California—a mountain-climbing future and a business future. His energetic character, like that of many of his contemporary San Franciscans, had been formed in New England. He spent his first childhood years in an atmosphere that mingled the firm discipline of tradition with the fresh perspectives of social and economic ferment.

George's parents, Christopher and Hepzibah Bayley, were both sixth-generation Americans. They were married in 1820 in Newburyport, Massachusetts.[2] George was the fifth child born to them. At his birth he represented more than two hundred years of maritime living in America, all of it on the New England coast. For five generations before his, the lines of his father's seafaring ancestors could be traced to American colonists who emigrated from England on sailing ships in the sixteen-hundreds.[3] George's mother's family had come across the ocean and settled in the New World at about the same time.[4] Behind her were Newbury and Newburyport landholders, church petitioners, Revolutionary War heroes, coopers, and mariners.

During colonial times, climbing in Newburyport, Massachusetts, meant scaling either church steeples or masts of ships. In bed recovering from childbirth, one of George's maternal ancestors watched through her window to see her husband, Samuel Pettingell, climb the steeple of the Old South Presbyterian

Church of Newburyport. One of the early petitioners for the privilege of forming the church and now owner of its covenant, he was helping with the building of the steeple, and he fell to his death before his wife's eyes.[5]

George's male paternal ancestors, including his father, were all seamen. In 1823, at the age of thirty-two, Christopher, George's father, became a ship's captain. By 1830 he had acquired and commanded several schooners in the West Indies molasses trade.[6] He and his wife had settled among the stately Federal and Georgian houses of Newburyport. While he sailed the seas, Hepzibah remained ashore and bore their three daughters, Charlotte, Elizabeth, and Caroline, one son who died when he was a child, and, in time, George.[7]

Three years before George was born, Captain Bayley left the ships and left Newburyport. For the hardworking Yankees, now citizens of the United States, shipbuilding, fishing, and foreign commerce had generated great wealth and the building of magnificent houses and churches. But Newburyport's golden age, which lasted from the Revolutionary War to the War of 1812, came to an end when the city's commerce fell victim to Jefferson's embargo, a destructive fire in 1811, and the War of 1812. During the clipper ship era, shipbuilding temporarily recovered, but the golden age had passed, and the young nation fell into a severe depression.

In 1837 Captain Bayley moved his wife and daughters to booming Boston.[8] Unaffected by the depression, Boston continued to grow and prosper. The port became the hub of a wide, intricate wheel of international distribution and finance. To this waterfront Christopher brought his family. He opened a tailor and draper's shop on the corner of Broad Street and Fort Hill Wharf. He settled the family only two blocks away at the corner of Pearl and Purchase streets. In this house, on April 27, 1840, George Blake Bayley was born.[9] His sisters were then eighteen, thirteen, and eight years old.[10]

The Boston in which George spent his first few years bore a strong physical resemblance to the San Francisco in which he was to settle twenty years later. Boston was still confined by water, and the spacious wharves occupied fully twenty percent of that area. Girdling the town like a jagged question mark, the wharves were visible from every part of Boston. Beyond the jumbled wooden and granite warehouses rose a forest of masts and canvas. The old salts who patronized Christopher Bayley's shop reeked of tar and molasses. Young George's pulse quickened at exotic tales of the silk potentates of Singapore, of the perils of whaling and Cape Horn—and of the gold rush fever in California. Yet the bustling, cosmopolitan waterfront in no way impinged on the contented stillness of the residential lanes that were only a block or two back from the water. Pearl Street, on which the Bayleys lived, was lined with fine old houses and spacious gardens that bloomed all summer. The custom of leaving the city during the summer months had not yet taken hold. Even the school in the neighborhood had hollyhocks that bloomed in their season.

As the 1850s approached, the city entered a period of rapid change. American sailing ships were yielding Atlantic trade supremacy to European steamships. Immigrants, including refugees from the Irish famine, began to arrive in large numbers, while thousands of "old colonials" were departing for New York, the Middle West, and the Far West. When commercial buildings and cheap boarding houses invaded the residential district of Fort Hill, social tensions mounted. Fort Hill was being overrun, and Christopher moved his family to Somerville, about five miles northeast of Boston.[11] Two years later he moved them again, farther north to the prim village of Medford.[12]

Young George had already known a rupture more painful than that of leaving Boston. At the age of four, before they left, he lost his mother.[13] The inscription on her gravestone pays her tribute that underlines the extent of his loss: "She was a faithful and affectionate wife, a tender mother, a sincere friend and Christian. She sleeps in Jesus and when He the Christian's hope and life appears, she shall be like Him, seeing Him as He is."[14]

Hepzibah's untimely death deprived not only the children of a mother and Captain Bayley of a wife, but also the large household of a manager. An 1840 census-taker had counted thirteen heads under the Bayley roof.[15] As was usual in those days, Christopher lost no time in filling the vacancy left by his wife's

death. Within five months of burying Hepzibah in the family
plot in Newbury, he married Livonia Sawyer.[16] He was fifty-
three, she thirty-eight.

A deeply religious woman, the daughter of a Congregationalist preacher, Livonia brought a spirit of orthodoxy into the
house. At a time when the old strictures of the Puritans and
Congregationalists were in retreat before the softening effects of
Unitarianism and romanticism, Livonia pressed her views so
insistently on her stepdaughters that she virtually drove them
out of the family home. Charlotte and her husband, taking
Caroline along, set sail for San Francisco when George was ten.[17]
By the following year, 1851, all three of his sisters had left home
and were married.[18]

Under Livonia's influence even Captain Bayley was trans-
formed from a quick-tempered, profane old seaman, who once
remarked of a bothersome customer in his draper's shop, "Fool,
doesn't know her ars from her elbow," into a God-fearing pa-
rishioner who sedately bowed the bass viol in the Medford Congregationalist church.

When George was six, Livonia gave birth to a son, Frank
Toppan Bayley.[19] Before long, Livonia brought her mother and
an orphaned nephew to join the household.[20] These additions
made the home more Sawyer than Bayley, more religious than
maritime. George's young, new half-brother was destined to become a Congregationalist minister and did.[21]

George received the classical schooling then highly prized by
families like his own. He had entered the world at a fascinating
time—near the midpoint of a period later dubbed the "New
England flowering." The era's best-known literary son, Ralph
Waldo Emerson, spoke warmly of the times: "The ancient manners were giving way. There grew a certain tenderness on the
people, not before marked." Yet flinty Yankee intellectualism,
practicality, and self-consciousness were still there, too. Emerson
added that "The young men were born with knives in their
brains."

According to the custom among New England lads, at the
age of fifteen George Bayley did what his father had done: he
went off to sea.[22] While young George was developing strength

and learning to accept discipline on the oceans, his father moved to Portland, Maine. There, as superintendent of a sailors' home, Christopher again set up a waterfront draper and tailor's shop. He advertised:

> *Cheap Cash Clothing Store,* a full assortment of Cloths of all kinds, of the best quality, including Pilot and Beaver Cloths, Doeskins, etc. Particular attention given to the cutting and making of all garments. . . . Ready made clothing of all kinds, constantly on hand. Also, the best kinds of oil clothing, double or single. Officers and Seamen furnished for Ships. Chronometers on hire.[23]

In 1857, when George had just turned seventeen, Christopher died at sixty-six of what was diagnosed as congestion of the brain.[24] Although his body was sent to Newbury to be interred next to George's mother,[25] the minister of the Portland mariner's church offered a eulogy that pointed up something of the heritage that equipped George for the sailor's life he had chosen and the pioneer life he was soon to choose.[26]

The Reverend Merrill said of Captain Bayley, of George's father:

> . . . one of the few who always came here to our solemn feasts. . . . Occupying an important and responsible position—as superintendent of the "Sailor's Home" in this city, having spent his best days among seamen—having passed through every grade from the lowest to the highest on shipboard—knowing the hearts and understanding well the privations, toils and hardships of seamen and ever anxious to meet their temporal and spiritual wants, many a sailor will feel that he has lost a friend. . . . He has spoken in his remembered words of warning and counsel to seamen amid the perils of the tempest, and when smitten of God and on the verge of death in foreign hospitals. . . .
>
> And may we not hope that he will meet with many a one in the port of eternal rest, conducted there by the pilot he so earnestly recommended?

George had never known his father as a sailor, but Captain Bayley remained a sailor's man to the end. His death gave finality to his son's New England life but would mark what six generations of colonial heritage had bestowed on the orphaned George for the unknown he faced ahead.

The year was 1857, just after the heyday of the legendary Yankee clipper ships. Although English iron steamships were successfully challenging New England's wood-and-canvas vessels in the European trade, New England's maritime empire had expanded to every corner of the earth. George had a part in that empire, and for seven years he coped with the foibles of the sea, its sailors, and their ships. The experience fortified the physical hardiness that was his Yankee birthright, and it nurtured his expansive love of the outdoors.

At twenty-two George stepped ashore in San Francisco, quitting the sea forever.[27] He moved in with his sister Caroline and her husband, Charles Story, whom she had married a year after coming west. Story had sailed from Salem, Massachusetts, around the Horn to San Francisco.[28] With sixty-four other forty-niners he had bought the barque *La Grange*. They sold the ship in Sacramento, after which it served as a prison for many miscreants of the gold rush influx.

George first found work at the San Francisco Sugar Refinery;[29] two years later he took a job as deputy tax collector under his brother-in-law.[30] As a pioneer in San Francisco, Story owned a drug supply business, became the city's license collector and then its tax collector.[31] The Storys lived on Bryant Street, on Rincon Hill.[32] Industry began to push up the hill toward the residences, just as it had done when the Bayleys lived on Fort Hill in Boston. The gravitation northward toward Nob Hill started, and the Storys moved across Market Street to McAllister Street, where they had a house built for them by H. L. King, the leading builder of the day.[33] Living with the Storys gave George Bayley instant social, business, and political status. The McAllister Street house was a center of warmth and gaiety, where the Chinese cook was always ready for fifteen or twenty to drop in for lunch.

Bayley had arrived in 1862, the same year that the San Francisco Stock Exchange first opened its doors. The city's frenetic early growth had leveled off during the fifties, as the waves of the rush for gold died away. But in the sixties San Francisco got a powerful second-stage boost from silver discoveries in Nevada's Comstock Lode. Much of the total wealth generated by that incredible bonanza came to be spent in the city by the Golden Gate. The millions needed to finance this and other industrial-age mining ventures throughout the West were largely funneled through San Francisco, solidly establishing it as a financial center. The era's precarious glories were summed up in the roller-coaster career of William Ralston, in whose Bank of California George Bayley—with his sure sense of adventure—later found work. Ralston assigned George to the job of bookkeeper.[34] But the excitement of social and business life in a city trading in gold and silver stocks, growing as a great port, worrying its own problems of gestation while the Civil War was going on elsewhere was not enough for George Bayley. He was hearing about other parts of California. San Franciscans were beginning to go camping south on the San Francisco peninsula or north in the Russian River valley, and a few ventured to vacation to the east in the Sierra.

During the fifties prospecting and gold mining provided tales and legends of life in California's foothills on the other side of the Great Valley. Overland caravans in Conestoga wagons brought with them stories of the dramas in the high mountains. Surveyors for a transcontinental railway recorded measurements and descriptions that made city dwellers aware that the great Sierra Nevada barrier was there.

In the sixties the Nevada silver mines lured more fortune seekers back across the 7,000-foot, snow-covered summit. The cross-country telegraph kept the west end as well as the east end of the continent in touch with new exploitations of mountain and river-bed lands. Concord stages from Sacramento to the mines made trafficking back and forth to San Francisco a regular thing. All these kinds of communication—and the completion of the overland railroad—made the threats and the majesty of the Sierra common knowledge.

The Yosemite, too, had been discovered and its beauty acknowledged. In 1864 Abraham Lincoln diverted his attention from the Civil War long enough to sign a bill prohibiting commercialization of a large area including the Yosemite Valley. From his reading, from his spot midst the hubbub of business, and from the other new San Franciscans he met socially, George learned of the majesty and challenge of the Sierra; and he wanted to see them.

Besides the desire he had the muscle. Seven years of scaling masts and setting rigging had built his agile, wiry body on its short frame to a physique of unusual strength. Small bones, sloping shoulders, a beard, and thinning hair deceived his associates. His joy at the deception sparked a continuing twinkle in his clear, blue, sailor's eyes. He always wanted to go to the top of the mast or the mountain to see the vistas in all directions and to look beyond the horizons. He had already savored the "spice of danger" on a mountain-top while he was climbing in New England. At the peak of Mount Washington in New Hampshire he had experienced a 105-mile-an-hour gale.[35] Now in the western landscape the Yosemite had become the premier symbol of purity, beauty, and challenge; and George was ready for it.

NOTES

1. *San Francisco Directory, 1862.*

2. *Vital Records of Newbury, Massachusetts to the End of the Year 1849* (Salem, Mass.: Essex Institute, 1911), Vol. II, *Marriages and Deaths,* p. 27.

3. Priscilla Willis, "Bayley Genealogy," Visalia, California, 1969 (unpublished) .

4. John Mason Pettingell, *A Pettingell Genealogy* (Boston: New England Genealogical Society, 1906), pp 46, 96, 97.

5. Pettingell, *A Pettingell Genealogy,* p. 47.

6. *Ship Registers of the District of Newburyport, Massachusetts, 1789-1870* (Salem, Mass.: Essex Institute, 1937) , pp. 93, 94, 233.

7. *Vital Records of Newbury, Massachusetts.*

8. *Simpson's Boston Directory, 1837.*

9. Monument, Mountain View Cemetery, Oakland, California.

10. *Vital Records of Newbury, Massachusetts.*

11. *U.S. Census, Somerville, Massachusetts, 1850.*

12. *Boston City Directory, 1852.*

13. "Deaths," *Boston Evening Transcript,* Vol. XV, No. 4277, July 1, 1844, p. 3.

14. Headstone, Old Burying Ground, Newbury, Massachusetts.

15. *U.S. Census, Boston, Massachusetts, 1840.*

16. Nathaniel Sawyier and Joseph Burbeen Walker, *A Genealogy of Some of the Descendants of William Sawyer of Newbury, Massachusetts,* (Manchester, N.H.: W. E. Moore, 1889).

17. *San Francisco County Census, July, 1852.*

18. Caroline P. Murman, "Charles Robinson Story," biographical notes, California Historical Society, San Francisco.

19. Sawyier and Walker, *A Genealogy.*

20. *U.S. Census, Somerville, Massachusetts, 1850.*

21. *Congregational Yearbook, 1917,* Congregational Library, Boston, p. 464.

22. "Mount Tacoma," *The Daily Oregonian* (October 1, 1833).

23. *Portland, Maine City Directory, 1856-1857,* p. 22.

24. "Deaths," *Portland Transcript,* May 16, 1857, p. 47.

25. Headstone, Old Burying Ground, Newbury, Massachusetts.

26. The Rev. Samuel H. Merrill, *The Blessed Dead: Discourse Occasioned by the Death of Capt. Christopher T. Bayley* (Randolph, Mass.: Samuel P. Brown, no date).

27. *San Francisco Directory, 1862.*

28. Caroline P. Murman, "Charles Robinson Story."

29. *San Francisco Directory, 1862.*

30. *San Francisco Directory, 1864-1865.*

31. Caroline P. Murman, "Charles Robinson Story."

32. *San Francisco Directory, 1864-1865.*

33. Caroline P. Murman, "Charles Robinson Story."

34. *San Francisco Directory, 1870.*

35. George Bayley, "Mount Takhoma," *Overland Monthly,* VIII (September, 1886), pp. 266–78.

CHAPTER FOUR

The Temple of Nature

FOUR HUNDRED THIRTY-EIGHT visitors penetrated the Yosemite Valley in the summer of 1866.[1] Among them were George Bayley and four friends from San Francisco: the brothers Charles and Horatio Livermore, Theodore E. Smith, and F. P. McMahon.[2] They all boarded a river steamer in San Francisco. At Benicia, the next stop up the bay, a young widow, Josephine Warren, joined them. She kept a journal of the adventure and rewrote it in narrative form after her return to her home in Connecticut. She recorded the events of the trip in charming, Victorian idiom. She presented the first comments available on George's reactions to the grandeur and challenges of the mountains, the first indication of the start of his pattern of going to Yosemite every summer.

Her journal begins under the date of June 9, 1866:

> After a long term of study and hard work, I made a sudden resolve, ere my departure for the Atlantic States . . . to see the far-famed "Big Trees"—of which I had read and heard so much and which in days past I had pictured in my "mind's eye" as marvelous and unreal. . . . But, *to see them*, I determined, and setting aside the discomforts which might attend me, alone, on such a trip, I found myself on Saturday, June 9th, 1866, at the hour of six P.M. surrounded by friends, on the dismal wharf at Benicia, awaiting the arrival of the ". . . . ." [riverboat].

Through the narrow passage which connects the Suisun

and San Pablo Bays, slowly steamed the looked-for boat. Soon she cast anchor alongside our wharf, when suddenly appeared to view, on the forward deck, faces familiar and friendly. As if an enchantment had burst upon me, I echoed back the words of those from whom I parted on shore. "Not alone." "Your friends are on board."

Oh, what magic in the sound of a familiar voice or in the clasp of a friendly hand. Was it not some good spirit that sent hither, on that same boat bound for Stockton, five noble, brave, true men, to protect me on my way?

How generously they offered me the *sixth* and vacant seat in their carriage, and how gratefully I accepted it, after having been fully assured that I, a lady, should not be an encumbrance to their party or detract from their preconceived plans of jollity and merriment.[3]

They steamed up the San Joaquin River to Stockton, disembarked, and spent the night there. The next morning they headed East in two horse-drawn vehicles, and they crossed the hot, dusty valley. Into the browning, oak-studded foothills they arrived in Copperopolis, a mining community which had boomed to two thousand persons during the recently ended Civil War. Through clear, unpolluted air, with the setting sun to their backs they could see what John Muir would come to call the "Range of Light." The six travelers saw the Sierra two years before John Muir first saw those mountains, ten years before he was to write about meeting George Bayley among their wonders.

After the adventurers spent a comfortable night in the hotel at Copperopolis, they traveled by wagon up several thousand feet to the beginning of the steeper mountains and evergreen trees and to the worked-out gold mining village of Murphys. That afternoon they climbed still higher. The road over the hills was bordered on either side with forests of huge pines, cedars, and firs, which somewhat prepared them for the greater dimensions of the Big Trees proper, the *sequoiae giganteae* which Mrs. Warren had set out to see. The travelers arrived at the imposing grove early in the evening to spend the night amid the giants. She recorded their climbing among the famous trees:

> We spent the early morning hours in wandering through
> the grove, climbing by means of ladders, upon the trunks of
> prostrate trees, exploring their inner caves, some of which
> contained lakes of water, large enough to row a good sized
> canoe on.
>
> Sunday midday we returned to Murphys, George and I
> bringing up the rear, on horseback, an hour later than the
> others. We trotted leisurely along, inhaling long draughts of
> fresh mountain air, and making the silence vocal with our
> effusions of poetry and of song.

At Murphys Mrs. Warren expected to leave the men, return
to San Francisco, and catch a ship to Connecticut. But to her
surprise and delight she learned:

> . . . my friends, who were "en route" to the "Yosemite
> Valley," generously and urgently extended to me a cordial
> invitation to *remain* a sixth member of their party and share
> in the greater enjoyments in prospect. . . . A scanty wardrobe
> was quite out of the question on so long a journey. Many ob-
> jections arose but were as quickly removed by the ingenuity
> of the gentlemen. The one great idea, the sight of the wonder-
> ful Yosemite Valley, under *such pleasant circumstances,* and
> my last, perhaps *only* opportunity, took possession of me, and
> I yielded.

Mrs. Warren easily met the standards of dress through a shop-
ping expedition in Sonora, a gold rush town to which they returned the next day. She needed a lady's garments that would
complement George's unpressed, coarse trousers, an open-
necked long sleeved shirt, and an unbuttoned, sturdy vest,
topped by a dark, misshapen, broad-brimmed felt hat, turned
up all around. With everyone outfitted they continued to Coul-
terville the following day and gave up the wagons. On horseback under the leadership of their knowledgeable guide,[4] A.
Tiscornia, they went on through country in which there were
no roads. Of the second day on this approach to their objective
Mrs. Warren wrote:

Among the companions of George B. Bayley, left, on his first trip to Yosemite Valley in June 1866 were Horatio Livermore, center, and Charles Livermore, right.

As we neared the Yosemite, the peculiarity of the Country, plainly told us that we were within the precincts of the marvelous and the sublime. For several miles huge boulders lay strewn about, in wild confusion. One singularly shaped rock, not far from the "trail" was scaled by the irresistible George and Charlie. . . .

The roar of many waters reached our ears and we knew that we were nearing the Merced [River]. The guide ordered a halt, tightened our saddle-girths, and we were soon slowly but surely, for our horses were well trained to mountain travel, making our steep and circuitous way to the valley. In three miles we made a descent of 4000 feet.

The first object that burst upon our eager gaze, was the dim and feathery spray of the "Bridal Veil" [Falls] in the distance on our right. . . .

It was nearly nightfall when we entered the precincts of this temple of nature. We halted on the banks of the Merced, dismounted, and offered up oblations at the very portals of the Sanctuary, by bathing our heated and dusty brows in the cool, crystal waters of this River.

Resuming our saddles, we followed the "trail" down the North side of the river to a ferry, where on a rude boat, propelled by ropes and pulleys we crossed. About five miles up the valley is "Hutchings' Hotel." This with another smaller one, both built of rough boards, are the only buildings in the Valley and the only appearances of civilization except a small Ranch farther up the Valley known as "Lamon's Ranch." [Now the site of the Ahwahnee Hotel.] Art has never reared structures or spanned the streams, or connected the lofty buttresses to mar the perfections of Nature, and may her holy temple never thus be desecrated.

Mrs. Warren made her plea for conserving the valley as it was, as nature had arranged it, as she had beheld it, as George Bayley and his friends had shown it to her before John Muir had ever seen the Yosemite.

The group found shelter for their stay in the valley at Hutchings' Hotel, a twenty-foot by sixty-foot, two-story, wooden building. Mrs. Warren and her escorts had rooms with muslin windows and muslin interior walls. The hospitality and location of the hotel within sight and sound of the never-ceasing pouring and music of Yosemite Falls compensated for the lack of privacy. Although the hotel was equipped to handle twenty-eight guests at the most, Mr. Hutchings could never refuse to make impossibilities possible. By the final night of the six travelers' stay, more than seventy people piled in to eat and sleep in improvised beds on the floors of the primitive building.

After a few days spent exploring the wonders of the floor and walls of the valley, the developing mountaineers went to the east end of the valley:

> John early prepared our horses, and we started in an easterly direction down to the lower extremity of the Valley. Another party joined us, but all except three fell out by the way.
>
> Following the Merced on its left bank for about five miles, we reached the point, where the valley separates into three canons, through each of which a stream flows to join the main Merced. The central canon is the principal one. By a wildly romantic trail, one sharp rock, and through tortuous windings closely obstructed by chaparral, we reached a point where we were obliged to dismount and pursue our course on foot. The Southern wall is here less perpendicular than elsewhere. The whole base consists of huge sharp boulders, which have crumbled from the sides and top of the wall. Trees grow from between the loose stones. Here and there fallen trunks, nearly obstruct the way—the whole mass of debris is thrown about in the grandest confusion. Over it all we scrambled and leaped and crawled. On our left the waters of the Merced formed a succession of beautiful cascades.

They faced a perpendicular wall of about 350 feet over which leaped the Vernal Fall.

> Continuing to the right through spray almost blinding, and over a steep ascent, saturated with mist, where on several

Hutchings' Hotel, where George B. Bayley and his party stayed in Yosemite Valley. (Photo courtesy U.S. National Park Service)

occasions we lost our foothold, we at last reached a rocky
ledge which served as a resting place for a time. By means of
several flights of almost perpendicular wooden steps, we
gained the summit of the "Vernal Fall." Thrown across the
very edge of the precipice, at the left of the Fall is a huge
natural parapet of granite. From this point we had a fine view
of this "Cataract of Diamonds" and of the cascades below.
Here, also, I experienced for the first time that beautiful
phenomenon, the "Circular Rainbow."

Above us the water rushed down from its never failing
source, over a rough bed, sometimes forming cascades and
anon gently spreading itself out like a huge apron over an
immense surface of smooth granite rock.

Our party ambitiously inclined pushed onward—over
masses of boulders and jagged rocks, and smooth water-worn
surfaces, until we reached a height exceeding that of "Nevada
Fall." George, Charlie, and McMahon rested not, until they
had scaled the loftiest point and stood far above the Nevada
Fall. A slide of fifty feet and four inches down the naked surface of a perpendicular rock did not even dampen the impetuosity of our friend George.

Indeed it did not dampen his impetuosity. On their final day
in Yosemite George achieved a new mountain-climbing feat:

Our last day in the "Valley" we concluded to pass within
sight of the matchless symmetry and beauty of the "Bridal
Veil." George and the guide chose to try new scenes and scaled
the cliffs to the foot of the Upper Yosemite....

Their stay at Hutchings' over, they started for home:

We left the Valley by the "Mariposa Trail" on the south
side of the Merced. In four miles we made an ascent of 4500
feet. From "Inspiration Point," which we reached by making
a detour from the "Trail" we caught our last views of the
Valley by looking *down*. Noble trees of 200 feet height, growing beside the river bank below, appeared as tiny shrubs. The

river, itself, looked, in its spiral course like a silvery thread. Away in the distance the summits of the Sierras lay clothed in eternal snows. The outside world had lost its charm, and we fain would have lingered in these wild recesses—but, the approaching midday sun warned us of the passing hours, and we resumed our saddles over steep grades, until at noon, we stopped beside a stream to "lunch." On the opposite bank lay a patch of snow—at a little distance. On our left, spread out with a rich green carpet, was a clearing of several acres over which sped a deer roused doubtlessly from his covert, by the report of a rifle, or perchance by McMahon's war-whoop.

A night spent at Clark's (now Wawona) , a ride to the Mariposa Grove of Big Trees, a couple of days spent getting to Stockton through Mariposa, and they were again on a riverboat down the San Joaquin River:

At midnight, our boat touched at Benicia and I parted from my traveling companions—happier and richer a hundred fold, than two weeks before, for all the experiences, the endearing friendships, the elevating hallowed memories of the time.

Never shall I cease to cherish the kindest regard, and the highest esteem for those five *gentlemen,* who are so thoroughly worthy the name in its highest sense, and to thank them with ever renewed expressions, for their kindness, generosity and courtesy to me.

So in 1866 George became the experimenting mountain climber among the group, the ebullient, agile, game one who always had his eye on the topmost spot. The trip had confirmed his yearning for mountains to climb. It had started his pattern of going to Yosemite every summer.

NOTES

1. J. M. Hutchings, *Heart of the Sierras, The Yo Semite Valley, Both Historical and Descriptive: And Scenes by the Way* (Yosemite Valley: Old

Cabin and Oakland, California: Pacific Press Publishing House, 1886), p. 130.

2. "Arrivals in Yosemite Valley," *Mariposa Gazette*, July 6, 1866, p. 2.

3. J. I. Warren, "The Yosemite," manuscript at Society of Pioneers, San Francisco, 1866.

4. *Grand Register of the Cosmopolitan*, at the Yosemite Museum, June, 1866.

CHAPTER FIVE

Yosemite Every Summer

THE YEAR FOLLOWING that habit-forming trip, 1867, George Bayley returned to Yosemite, again accompanied by a lady, a different lady—his wife.[1]

On August 7, 1867, he married Gertrude Arthur in San Francisco.[2] The intrepid George could not have chosen a more suitable wife to share his passion for getting to the top. Like George, Gertrude was short, compact, and strong. She complemented his impetuosity with a quiet dignity and containment, both of which could be compromised when she responded to George's demands to go along wherever he wanted. George married Gertrude in her church, the First Presbyterian Church of San Francisco. His bride was the spunky daughter of John D. Arthur, a forty-niner who had sailed around the Horn on the ship *Samoset* from his New York birthplace.[3] He and his son were San Francisco's pioneer agricultural implement and hardware merchants.[4] Mr. Arthur had joined the Presbyterian church and become an elder while services were still being held in a tent.

George and Gertrude Bayley spent a unique honeymoon in George's developing world of mountain climbing. They were not the first San Franciscans to spend their wedding trip relishing the rigors and seeing the wonders of Yosemite. There had been others who spent their honeymoon there. But the Bayleys' wedding trip was different. Unlike William Ralston's nine years earlier, in which the flamboyant banker had taken along with his bride eight of the fourteen members of his wedding party—

all on horseback, all to camp out by the banks of the Merced River—George's honeymoon was private.[5] Just Gertrude and he, led by James Wilmer of Mariposa, a professional guide, made the trip. What gave distinction to the Bayleys' honeymoon were the mountain-climbing achievements of the bride and groom. On this, their first trip to the Yosemite together, George and Gertrude conquered the top of Nevada Falls, the top of Sentinel Rock, the trip up Indian Canyon, the top of Upper Yosemite Falls, and the top of North Dome.

Their wedding had been on Wednesday. They started their honeymoon by riverboat from San Francisco to Stockton. They went on by wagon to the road's end in the foothills, and from there they traveled by horseback over the mountains into the valley. They arrived in Yosemite on the Monday following their wedding.

On Tuesday their climbing started with a ride up the river to the easily accessible Vernal Falls, where George had been the year before. They saw what John Muir described as "a staid, orderly, graceful, easy going fall proper and exact in every movement and gesture."[6] Riding up the valley another mile, the Bayleys dismounted and climbed a good deal higher. They climbed to a point above the Nevada Falls where George had slid the year before. They commanded a view of whitened water plunging six hundred feet to the valley below them. They beheld the river far below, the glacier-built walls on either side, and the bulk of Glacier Point Ridge in front of them. In this setting Mrs. Bayley claimed title as the third woman who had ever been to the top of the Nevada.

On Wednesday George took his bride to the foot of Yosemite Falls. They looked up over two thousand feet at the grandeur of the lower and upper falls displaying themselves as one. The comet-like masses of water tempted them to get somehow to the top of the roaring tandem, never mind how many thousands of feet up nor how steep the climb. George Bayley determined to get to the top later in the week, after a few less demanding feats had been accomplished.

Thursday George's bride followed him to the very top of Sentinel Rock. Here he led her to the triumph that put her

Sentinel Rock in Yosemite, where George B. Bayley took his bride on their honeymoon. Mrs. Bayley was the first woman to climb to the top of Sentinel Rock. (Photo courtesy California Historical Society Library)

Yosemite Falls. The Bayleys camped at the top. (Photo courtesy California Historical Society Library)

name in mountain-climbing records. She was the first woman ever to reach the top of the towering 3,000-foot obelisk. At least until 1886 no other woman even attempted the ascent of the difficult and dangerous monument.[7] But on their honeymoon in 1867 George and his bride stood on the highest point of Sentinel Rock, placed a white flag that remained until it waved into shreds, and inscribed a lead plate, which they left on one of the two pine trees that grew on the rock. Descriptions of explorations in the Yosemite and guidebooks ever since that date have credited the remarkable lady with her accomplishment.

Friday their guide led them to Mirror Lake to see the imposing presences of Half Dome and Mount Watkins reflected in the glassy, dark water. They had departed their hotel early in the morning, had ridden their horses a few miles up the river to the lake, and had arrived before the sun was on the water, while reflections were exact images of what they could see above.

For Saturday night George planned an overnight camp-out, the excursion to conquer a route to the top of those ever-appealing, frightening Upper Yosemite Falls. Their guide sent an Indian around the route they would take with what the guide called "camping necessaries." Then the guide led his enthusiasts up the valley to the more northerly Indian Canyon. Leaving their horses, they climbed the rugged canyon, breaking trail to Yosemite Creek far above the falls, and followed the stream down to the top of the Upper Yosemite Falls and their campsite. They were 2,640 feet above the floor of the valley, standing above both of the falls to behold from that vantage the spectacle of the valley, its cliffs, its peaks, its other waterfalls, and its poetry and music. Their campfire became an answering signal to a surveyor's fire atop Sentinel Dome, directly across the valley in full view of the Bayley lookout point.

Sunday they went to the even more dramatic higher cliff on the east side of the fall and planted another flag and inscription. Then on they went up North Dome to put up yet another banner. Thirty-four years later, in the summer of 1901, one of the three lead plates showing what the Bayleys had accomplished was found atop North Dome by a guide.[8] Clearly engraved on the flattened piece of lead was, "George B. Bayley, Mrs. Ger-

*North Dome, Yosemite, which the Bayleys also climbed in 1867.
(Photo courtesy California Historical Society Library)*

trude Bayley, San Francisco; Jas. H. Wilmer, guide, Mariposa; ascended Indian Canon 1867." Evidence of their record remained, although subsequent climbers knew nothing about it.

The only one of these firsts to be found in the old records of the valley was that of Mrs. Bayley's having been the first woman to reach the top of Sentinel Rock. George took great satisfaction in leaving his name on the summits he conquered, but he sought no applause from the public who did not follow him to those almost impossible heights. He sought no notice after he came down.

From North Dome they hiked northeast until they struck the Mono Trail above the far head of the valley, where they beheld the colossus of Mount Clark. Again, George's lady was the first, the first woman ever to go down the Mono Trail, ever to see Mount Clark from the point where the best view of it was found. There they met the waiting horses, and the three climbers all had the energy to gallop down the valley to their hotel.

Monday the bride and groom and their guide rested. The dramatic climbs had been accomplished, the flags flown, and the records set. Tuesday they quietly visited Illilouette Falls, rounding out their visits to the major waters that pour over the cliffs of the valley walls.

On Wednesday they left the valley. Their trip prompted Mr. Wilmer, the guide, to understate his admiration in a newspaper piece for the *Mariposa Gazette*. He noted, "They proved themselves capable of enjoying the trip more than most visitors." And he commented further that he thought this trip to be the most pleasant he had made to Yosemite. For George these pleasures continued a pattern of life—his pattern of visiting Yosemite every summer.

In San Francisco George and Gertrude lived with the Arthur family in their house on Bush Street.[9] There the newlyweds stayed until a new house was ready for them across San Francisco Bay in Oakland. As George's interest in mountaineering and in his job in San Francisco continued and developed, another one came along, and during the decade of the seventies it led him to enter a third arena.

A technological revolution was transforming agriculture and animal husbandry from the occupations of a medieval peasant into those of a modern business manager. George's part in that revolution—his part in initiating the work that would eventually make California the number one agricultural state in the world's number one agricultural nation—commenced in 1870, the same year he moved his growing family to the full square block he bought in Oakland.[10] There he established, along with his home, a fancy poultry breeding and importing business. From New York, New Jersey, Montreal, and Boston he brought in top-quality stock—all surviving the trip on the brand new transcontinental railroad. He imported Brahmas, Houdins, and Cochins, and he introduced the first white-egg-laying White Leghorns, those prolific hens that are still the egg-raisers' favorite.

The lead article on the front page of the January 13, 1872 issue of San Francisco's *Pacific Rural Press* described Bayley's contribution in importing and developing the White Leghorns.

> Mr. Bayley's experience with the breed is that they mature more rapidly than any other fowl; at three months they are perfect epitomes of the old ones, and begin to lay at five months. In his opinion they are very well adapted to the wants of the farmers on this coast, owing to their hardiness, as they are not affected by the wet weather and cold winds. . . . The young are easy to rear; they feather up soon and when two months old are as sprightly as many chicks at four months of age. The hens are considered excellent winter layers, and will lay as large a number of eggs in a year as any fowls known. . . . They are medium-sized fowl of a quiet and docile disposition.
>
> Mr. Bayley has sent a few lots to Australia and quite a number to Honolulu; they stood the sea voyage well. The fact of this breed being somewhat cheaper than other fancy fowls will assist in commending them to farmers who wish to keep them for profit.[11]

Bayley's prediction that these Leghorns would succeed, as

George B. Bayley in 1871.

Gertrude Arthur, whom Bayley married August 7, 1867, in San Francisco.

well as his prophecy of an explosive demand for fine poultry in California, proved to be accurate when, during the seventies, the Bay Area attracted thousands of people.

Early articles giving details of Bayley's methods, yard arrangements, and variety of poultry sparked some lively and revealing correspondence between him and the *Rural Press* readers. One correspondent had visited Bayley's yard and praised its "order, neatness, cleanliness, thoroughbred stock, strong and healthy," his separate pens and perfect system.[12] But the visitor was appalled by the prices.

Bayley's reply a week later included not only an explanation of the prices but also a lot of Yankee wisdom and business acumen:

> I can assure the gentleman that had he to go to the bottom of his pocket as many times as I did, before reaching the "perfect system" which he admired, he would have found the "awful prices" to be on the other side of the ledger.
>
> I contend that it is utterly impossible to raise fine stock of any kind that is to be used to improve, invigorate and build up anew, as it were, a whole race, and sell it cheap, and I would shun upon principle, any person offering to sell a cheap fowl, taking it for granted that he had not what he pretended to have; not that I contend for fancy prices, but to do the subject justice, one must devote a great deal of time and attention to the selection of fowls that will breed well together, new blood must be had continually and great care must be taken that no bad bird be admitted to the flock as one such bird will spoil a whole season's chicks—producing such birds as the breeder could not conscientiously sell. There is vast difference between farmers selling to each other and a breeder who devotes his time to studying and improving the breeds selling to them, as they rely upon him to give them something which stands at the head of its class, and as a matter of course expect to pay for its superiority.[13]

During these first years Bayley took personal care of the yard himself, all the while commuting by ferry to his job in the city.[14]

Soon the yard was honeycombed with pens and crowded with prancing prizewinners scratching among the grasses for grain.

Within three years he added top-quality turkeys to his catalog. He brought West and introduced with great acclaim the giant-breasted Bronze Turkey.[15] His gobbler named "Colossus" weighed forty-two pounds. His advertisements in the *Pacific Rural Press* touted the quality of all his various birds.[16]

The cluckings, gobblings, and aroma issuing from the back of the Bayleys' square block in Oakland somewhat mellowed the formal mood of their gracious home on the front of the block.[17] But inside the bay-windowed, white, Italianate house there was visually little of the rural atmosphere inherent in such proximity to a poultry yard. Mrs. Bayley performed her role as mistress of the well-appointed two-story, Victorian house with great competence and dignity. Twice daily that dignity bent a little and her spunk triumphed, as morning and evening she drove her husband behind a team of spirited horses to and from the ferry slip for his commute to the city.[18]

In the early seventies George had changed his San Francisco job from assistant tax collector to bookkeeper at Ralston's Bank of California.[19] In the spring of 1875 the bank found itself in precarious straits. In August it failed, causing William Ralston's apparent suicide. Nonetheless, nimble-footed, nimble-spirited George soon landed a position as note-teller at San Francisco's Bank of Nevada, an institution newly founded by Ralston's arch-rivals: Flood, Fair, MacKay, and O'Brien, the Comstock bonanza kings.[20]

The job required George to handle and record the details of the bank's loans and the collateral put up as security for them.[21] He made collections of both interest and principal, and he accepted and stored gold bullion. His integrity was on display. There were no audits except his own. He also registered mining stocks and bank notes, keeping track of fifty or sixty of these items a day. His job not only provided a steady income but also figured in the big business deals that were going on, and it kept him well informed in many financial areas.

At the same time he was solidifying his position in various cultural facets of society. He joined the embryo San Francisco

The officers and staff of the Bank of California, 1874, in the directors' room. William C. Ralston, president, is seated in the center under the portrait of Darius Mills. The black arrow points to George B. Bayley, seated. (Photo courtesy the California State Library, Sacramento)

Art Association and began to acquire contemporary paintings; most of them were of the mountain landscapes he loved so well.[22] During his years in Oakland he collected works of Keith, Yelland, Munger, Travernier, and Rix.[23] George was among the second wave of members in the city's now famed Bohemian Club.[24] It was a wave consisting not of esthetic "bohemians" like the first, but of harder-headed types interested in the arts, who could pay their dues, rescue the club from its financial crisis, and manage the resulting bank account. Appropriately, George Bayley was made the club's treasurer soon after he joined.

Neither imminent bank failure nor the demands of moonlighting in the poultry business crowded out Bayley's annual summer trips to the Yosemite during those early seventies. He became less and less alone in his curiosity and knowing about Yosemite. James Hutchings, who had settled in the valley in 1869, publicized its magnificence in his *California Magazine;* Albert Bierstadt came west to paint it, and Eadweard Muybridge to photograph it. A trickle of tourists ventured in to Hutchings' Hotel and gazed up at the awesome cliffs and roaring waterfalls. Geologist Clarence King had explored and described the Sierra Nevada range, giving special attention to the wonder of Yosemite.

The pattern George established on his honeymoon continued every summer, and he conquered at least one new peak a year. In 1873 in the Grand Register of the Cosmopolitan, that combination saloon, billiard hall, bath house, and barbershop, he modestly signed the register, "Returning from Mt. Lyell."[25] He documented not the first but *one* of the first ascents of that "inaccessible pinnacle," as Whitney called it.

As a regular visitor and climber, Bayley became acquainted with the guides and hotel keepers in the valley. He had met A. Tiscornia, who had guided him, his four friends, and Josephine Warren in 1866;[26] and he met J. M. Hutchings, in whose hotel he had stayed nearly every year since 1866. Later he came to know Charles Peregoy, whom George described as an unequaled camp cook and to whom George took a fine hotel register for the opening of Peregoy's short-lived Mountain View House.[27] And now he was to meet John Muir.

NOTES

1. James H. Wilmer, "Wanderings in Yo Semite Valley," *Mariposa Gazette,* September 14, 1867, p. 2.

2. "Marriages," *San Francisco Bulletin,* August 8, 1867.

3. Records at Mountain View Cemetery, Oakland, California.

4. "The Death of John D. Arthur on Tuesday Evening," *The Morning Call,* Vol. LXV, No. 62, January 31, 1889, p. 7.

5. Sarah Haight, "Diary," Manuscript at California State Library, Sacramento, California.

6. John Muir, *The Yosemite,* Natural History Library (Garden City, N.Y.: Doubleday, 1962) , p. 23.

7. J. M. Hutchings, *Heart of the Sierras, The Yo Semite Valley, Both Historical and Descriptive: And Scenes by the Way* (Yosemite Valley: Old Cabin and Oakland, Calif.: Pacific Press Publishing House, 1886) , p. 414.

8. *Mariposa Gazette,* July 6, 1901, p. 3.

9. *San Francisco Directory, 1870.*

10. "Poultry Notes, Choice Poultry Yards," *Pacific Rural Press,* March 25, 1871, p. 185.

11. "White Leghorn Fowls," *Pacific Rural Press,* Vol. III, No. 2, January 13, 1872, p. 1.

12. M. Eyre, Jr., "Poultry Notes: Practical Poultry Growing," *Pacific Rural Press,* March 1, 1873, p. 137.

13. George Bayley, "Thoroughbred Poultry," *Pacific Rural Press,* March 8, 1873, p. 153.

14. "Poultry Notes, Choice Poultry Yards," *Pacific Rural Press,* March 25, 1871, p. 185.

15. "The Bronze Turkey," *Pacific Rural Press,* April 5, 1873, p. 217.

16. Advertisement, *Pacific Rural Press,* January 11, 1873, p. 32.

17. Sketch by Geoffrey Bangs, son of a friend of Bayley's who boarded at the house.

18. Interview with Bayley's grandson, Lionel Bayley King.

19. *San Francisco Directory, 1872.*

20. *San Francisco Directory, 1877.*

21. Interview with Frederick L. Lipman, former Chairman of the Board of Wells Fargo Bank (successor to Bank of Nevada) , at History Room, Wells Fargo Bank, San Francisco.

22. *Constitution, Bylaws, List of Members, Catalogue of Library and Rules of the School of Design of the San Francisco Art Association,* San Francisco, 1878, p. 38.

23. Final Accounting of Will of Gertrude Bayley King (Bayley's daughter) (Alameda County Court House, Oakland, California, 1918) .

24. *Annals of the Bohemian Club,* San Francisco, 1880, Vol. 1, p. 186.

25. *Grand Register of the Cosmopolitan,* Yosemite Museum, July 20, 1873.

26. "Arrivals in Yosemite Valley," *Mariposa Gazette,* July 6, 1866, p. 2.

27. *Hotel Register, Mountain View House,* June 26, 1874.

CHAPTER SIX

Mountains Are Fountains

IT WAS INEVITABLE that on his expeditions in the Yosemite Bayley should befriend John Muir, the young Scot who, on first witnessing Yosemite Valley, had exulted, "Born again!"[1] Muir had become a fixture there in 1868.[2] Although the first mention of George Bayley in Muir's writings occurred seven years after Muir's arrival, surely they had met well before that.

Muir first named Bayley as a companion in a lengthy account of the 1875 trip they made together from Yosemite through the Kings River Valley[3] and to the top of Mount Whitney.[4] They came back to the Yosemite by Mono Pass, Mono Lake, and Bloody Canyon.[5] The account of that trip, taken just before the Bank of California's failure, was printed in the San Francisco *Daily Evening Bulletin* shortly after the bank failed.

Only four men, including the mule-master and Muir himself, set out on the trip. Muir wrote of the expedition and of Bayley:

> We set out from here [Yosemite] on the 9th of July, our party consisting of George Bayley of San Francisco, Charles Washburn, a student of the State University, with "Buckskin Bill" as mule master, all well mounted on tough, obstinate mules. Right gladly we pushed our way into the wild untrampled kingdom of the Sierra, inspired with the thousand indefinite joys of the green summer woods; past Clark's Station [Wawona] and the Mariposa Grove of Big Trees; through luxuriant forests of the Upper Fresno, fairly drip-

ping with balsam and gum; climbing many a hill and dale
bestrewn with brown burs, and fording many a bright dashing brook edged with tangled alders and willows; making a
devious trail, yet tending ever southward, independent in our
course as birds in the calm cloudless air. . . .

Of Bayley's behavior as he discovered the beauties in the
Kings River Canyon Muir wrote:

Bayley's joy usually finds expression in a kind of explosive
Indian war whoop, and wild echoes were driven rudely from
cliff to cliff, as the varied landscapes revealed themselves from
the more commanding points along the trail.

And farther on, as they faced Mount Whitney, Muir again
commented on the habit Bayley had acquired:

Men ascend mountains as instinctively as squirrels ascend
trees, and of course, the climbing of Mount Whitney was a
capital indulgence, apart from the enjoyment drawn from
landscapes and scientific pursuits. We set out from the little
village of Independence with plenty of excelsior determination, Bayley as usual, rejoicing in war-whoops much to the
wonderment of sober passers-by.

At the start up Mount Whitney Muir approved of Bayley's
equipment:

Each carried a loaf of bread, a handful of tea and a tincup,
and a block of beef about four inches in diameter, cut from
the lean heartwood of a steer; the whole compactly bundled
in half a blanket, and carried by a strap passed over the
shoulder, and beside these common necessaries, Bayley carried a small bottle of spirits for healing, sustaining and forti-
fying uses, in case of encounters with triangular headed
snakes, bears, Indians, mountain rams, noxious night airs,
snow storms, etc.; and in case of vertigo and difficult breath-
ing at great heights, together with broken bones, flesh wounds,

skin erosions, abrasions, contusions. For in prudence, is it not well to realize that "something might happen," and well to have a helpful spirit—a guardian angel in a bottle ever near?

Of Bayley's abandon and its possible consequences Muir noted:

Here occurred the only accident worth mentioning connected with the trip. Washburn, who climbs slowly, was soon considerable distance to the rear, and I sat down at the head of the narrow gully to wait for him. Bayley soon came up somewhat breathless with exertion, and without thinking of consequences, loosened a big boulder that went bounding down the narrow lane with terrible energy, followed by a train of small stones and dust. Washburn was about a hundred feet below, and his destruction seemed inevitable, as he was hemmed in between two sheer walls not five feet apart. We shouted to give him warning, and listened breathlessly until his answering shout assured us of his escape. On coming up weary and nerve-shaken with fright, he reported that the dangerous mass shot immediately over him as he lay crouched in a slight hollow. Falling rocks, single or in avalanches, form the greatest of all the perils that beset the mountaineer among the summit peaks.

Although Muir did not yet feel the admiration he later expressed for Bayley's mountain-climbing prowess and successes, there was evidence that it was developing when he wrote of the climb to the dividing ridge and on toward the top of the peak:

We followed the snow nearly to its upper limit, where it leaned against the dividing axis of the range, placing our feet in hollows melted by radiated heat from stones shot down from the crumbling heights. To scale the dividing ridge in front was impossible, for it swept aloft in one colossal wave with a vertical shattered crest. We were therefore compelled to swerve to the north; then carefully picking our way from ledge to ledge, gained the summit about 8 A.M. There stood

Mount Whitney now without a single ridge between; its
spreading base within a stone's throw; its pointed, helmet-
shaped summit 2,000 feet above us. We gazed but a moment
on the surrounding grandeur; the mighty granite battle-
ments; the dark pine woods far below, and the glistening
streams and lakes; then dashed adown the western slope into
the valley of the Kern.

On my first ascent I pushed direct to the summit up the
north flank, but the memories of steep slopes of ice and snow
over which I had to pick my way, holding on by small points
of stones frozen more or less surely into the surface, where a
single slip would result in death, made me determine that no
one would ever be led by me through the same dangers. I
therefore led around the north base of the mountain to the
westward, much to Bayley's disgust, who declared that he
could, or at least *would* follow wherever I was able to lead. . . .
I remained firm in avoiding the dangerous ice slopes.

Bayley soon proved that by comparison he was a seasoned
climbing companion:

We passed along the rocky shores of a lake whose surface
was still (July 21st) covered with cakes of winter ice, around
the edges of which the color of the water was a beautiful
emerald green. Beyond the lake we gradually climbed higher,
mounting in a spiral around the northwest shoulder of the
mountain, crossing many a strong projecting buttress and
fluting hollow, then bearing to the left urged our way directly
to the summit. Higher, higher, we climbed with muscles in
excellent poise, the landscape becoming more and more glori-
ous as the wild Alps rose in the tranquil sky.

Bayley followed closely, lamenting the absence of danger,
whenever in this attenuated air he could command sufficient
breath. Washburn seldom ventured to leap from rock to rock,
but moved mostly on all fours, hugging projecting angles and
boulders in a sprawled, outspread fashion like a child clinging timidly to its mother, often calling for directions around
this or that precipice, and careful never to look down for fear

of giddiness, yet from first to last evincing a most admirable
determination and persistence of the slow and sure kind.
Shortly after 10 o'clock A.M. we gained the utmost summit—
a fact duly announced by Bayley as soon as he was rested into
a whooping condition, and before any note was taken of the
wilderness of landscapes by which we were zoned.

We left the summit about noon and swooped to the torrid
plains before sundown, as if dropping out of the sky.

Muir's developing respect for Bayley as a mountaineer began
to show in Muir's generalizations about the potential of man:

In every country the mountains are fountains, not only of
rivers but of men. Therefore we all are born mountaineers,
the offspring of rock and sunshine; and, although according
to ordinary commercial methods of computation it may seem
a long way down through lichen and pine tree to God-like
human beings, yet measured by other standards the distance
becomes scarcely appreciable.

The last of Muir's series of articles described where they went
when they resumed their horses and what they saw. They rode
to the remains of Fort Independence, the lava floods of the
Owens Valley, and the green flats of Long Valley. They passed
the black lava and pinnacles of the Inyo Range, the "commanding form" of Mount Ritter, and the Minarets.

It could have been that year while Bayley was in these mountains that he achieved the top of the almost inaccessible peak
in the Inyo Range that he and John Muir named the "California Matterhorn."[6] In his *Overland Monthly* account of his
first trip to the summit of Mount Rainier, Bayley described the
challenge as the only "real sample of looking destruction in the
face" that he experienced among the list of western peaks he
had conquered. The name "Matterhorn" recently has been
taken to identify a peak on another side of the valley. According
to Muir's biographers, his and Bayley's Matterhorn was either
what is known now as Rodgers Peak, or it was Banner Peak,
both of which are very near Mount Ritter.[7]

Although the account of the trip to Kings Canyon and Mount Whitney does not, nor does any other account, include a report of Bayley's conquest of the Matterhorn, this trip either recalled it, included it, or whetted Bayley's appetite for it. Among Muir's unpublished journals are some lines written in 1873 that detail his climb to the top of the Matterhorn and give definition to Bayley's phrase, "looking destruction in the face." Muir set out one morning to conquer the Matterhorn:

> Arrived at the summit after a stiff climb over neves and glaciers and loose, rocky taluses, but alack! the Matterhorn was yet miles away and fenced off from the shattered crest I was on, by a series of jagged, unscalable crests and glaciers that seemed steeper and glassier than any I had seen. After studying the situation like a chessboard, narrowly scanning each spiky wall and its glacier-guarded base. I made up my mind to the unhappy opinion that it would be wrong to incur so many dangers in seeking a way from this direction to the peak of Matterhorn. I concluded to spend the day with three glaciers to the left towards Ritter, and seek the Matterhorn again next day by ascending a canyon leading up from the north.[8]

To see better the jagged, zigzag topography, he scaled a 12,000-foot peak to his left. From there he determined to descend to one of the glaciers and climb through a narrow slot three or four feet wide into what promised to be a canyon leading to a neve that would meet a spur that would take him to the real summit. Seeing the way inspired him to go on:

> It is hard to give up a brave mountain, like the Matterhorn that you have counted on for years, and the upshot of this new view was that I began to scramble down towards the first glacier that lay beneath me, reached it, struck my axe into its snow, and found it in good condition—crisp, yet not too hard. There were some crevasses that threatened, and in some places the schrund yawned in what is called a cruel and infernal manner, but I escaped all these, passing the schrund by

a snow-bridge, and reached the narrow gap. There I found, to my delight, I could clamber down the south side, and that after I reached the edge of a little lake in which snowbergs were drifting, the rest of the way to the Matterhorn peak was nothing but simple scrambling over snow slopes over the snout of the Matterhorn glacier, across moraines, down the faces of fissured precipices, up couloirs threatened with avalanches of loose stones, on up higher, higher, peaks in crowds rising all around. . . . I reached the top-most stone.

The Matterhorn is built of black slate, blacker slate, and gray granite, mingled and interfused and belted and conglomerated, making a strange-appearing section on the slate in crack-like seams. In other places it appears to have got into large solid slate masses, like plums into a pudding. In some places the slate and granite seem to be about equal in quantity, and even mixed in the form of boulders, but planes of cleavage run unbrokenly through both slate and granite.

Whether George Bayley was along on Muir's 1873 climb of the "Matterhorn," or whether George climbed in 1875 or some other time, the threats remained identical, and climbing techniques employed no more tools nor any less ingenuity. On some trip Bayley hoodwinked the destructive force of the "California Matterhorn."

On this trip with Muir he had at least seen the challenging edifice, and then they had gone on to the Mono Basin and to Mono Lake. Exploring the lake provided the travelers with some added drama. Muir did not mention the experience in his newspaper articles. Undated notes among his unpublished journals play down the hair-raising experience. With emphasis heavily toward an appreciation of the wonders of nature, Muir recounted their exploration of the lake:

The party of three that I led through the pass to Mono Lake, were eager to sail its heavy waters and visit the islands. We borrowed an old water-logged boat from a nomad who was stopping there for a while. He cautioned us against delaying our return, as stormy winds often raised a heavy sea. . . .

The lake was calm, lying like a sheet of molten metal—a dead lake in every sense. We paddled gently, rambling along the white shore curves, careful not to overbalance the clumsy craft that seemed trying to turn turtle.

A sail on the lake develops a group of pictures of rare beauty and grandeur. Long ranks of snowy swans on the dark water, clouds of ducks enveloped in silvery spangles. The mighty barren Sierra rising abruptly from the waters to a height of seven thousand feet, and stretching north and south for twenty miles with rows of snowy peaks. Ranges of cumulus clouds swelling in massive bosses of pearl—cloud-mountains and rock mountains equally grand and substantial in appearance. Snow fields and ice in the higher hollows, white torrents dashing down shadowy groves, and smooth moraine slopes drawn out upon the gray sage plains along the base of the range, with silvery streams descending in bright cheery song to vanish in the dry desert.

The larger island in the lake is about two and a half miles long, and is composed of hard lava and loose ashes. The smaller, half a mile long with a cone two hundred and forty feet high, is of hard black lava, quite recent. Boiling springs and hot jets of gas boil up from the lake-bottom near its shore.

In two hours we gained the larger island and wandered about looking at the cone basalt, lavas, hot springs, and vegetation. . . . A few white and blue gulls slowly winnowed the air on the way to their homes, while here and there the swift wing of a swallow was seen.

Then clouds began to settle low on the dark cluster of peaks about Mount Ritter and at the head of Rush Creek, allowing the hacked summits to appear free above them. Mount Dana had a round gray cloud-cap which at first lightly touched, then gently clasped his snowy head. Heavy cumuli gathered and grew to the northeastward toward Aurora, and shadows crept across the gray levels about the lake.[9]

Nature changed its mood, and no longer could Muir's description outweigh the action dictated by circumstances and the other sailors:

Suddenly, at noon, a breeze fell from the mountains which soon roused the sleeping waters into white-crested waves.

Then we made haste to get back to the mainland, a distance of about seven miles from the island. After rowing hard and going about a third of the way, the wind began to blow in heavy surges that lashed the lake into a fierce roaring tempest. Water poured over the boat, faster than we could bail it out. Fearing we should sink, we turned back to the island, glad to get ashore anywhere. The waves broke unweariedly on the sloping beach.... I advised waiting patiently until the next day, but my comrades, hungry and without blankets, began to murmur. However, they submitted and went to bed, but the fire of slight brush could not be kept up and the cold made them shiver, causing them to roam in the darkness along the desolate shore, back and forth, like restless ghouls. They seemed to fear their lives were in danger, and they must escape at any risk, and gradually worked themselves up to a determined struggle for life, though the only danger lay in seeking to leave the island. At length, after midnight, they could no longer be restrained, and as the wind had slightly abated, I consented to try. We launched in safety and on we sped, keeping the boat squarely in the face of the wind to avoid upsetting. I, as pilot, sat in the bow to give warning of larger waves, one of my companions steered, and the other two rowed.

But, dangers or no dangers, Muir, like Bayley, remembered to note the mood of his environment:

Seven miles to go.... The range to the south loomed dim and vast, and along the shore the Indians had built large encircling brush fire fences, for it was sage rabbit hunting time. These made a livid illumination, and dense black clouds of smoke were seen rising, making one think that after centuries of repose the volcanic cones were again bursting into action.

The wind howled, the waves broke repeatedly, and we had to bail to keep afloat. I sat with shoes unlaced, ready to swim,

and feared not for life, as the water was not cold, though the
dashing of bitter spray would be trying to the eyes. . . .
Towards morning we got ashore and back to our camp in
an old abandoned hut in the possession of wood rats. Yet it
was a house, and all city visitors must have a roof over their
heads. . . .

Three years later Bayley himself published an account of another trip through most of the same country and told his version
of the near catastrophe on Mono Lake that he and Muir and
Washburn survived. More preoccupied with the drama of living, yet still aware of the beauties of nature, Bayley's memories
of the trip were different. In his twice-published 1878 journal,
entitled "Eleven Days in the High Sierra," he described his 1875
expedition on the lake. He reminisced:

As an account of the adventure may be a warning to other
venturesome tourists, I may be pardoned the digression to
narrate briefly one of the most thrilling episodes of a somewhat checkered life. Our party at the time consisted of four
gentlemen, one of whom was a geologist well known in California, whose tender love for nature has earned for him the
appellation of "the Thoreau of the Pacific."
In the course of our wanderings we found ourselves one
July day at the ranch of Louis Sammon, on the western shore
of Mono Lake. Having expressed a desire to visit the islands
in the lake, Louis Sammon volunteered us the use of an old
flat-bottomed boat and his company as guide. When we
started out in the morning the lake was calm, and we had a
pleasant row of six miles to one of the islands that seemed to
rest upon the water the perfect semblance of a turreted moni-
tor. Its surface was covered with lava, sand, ashes and pumice-
stone, and seemed fairly alive with gulls, whose eggs were
scattered over the ground by thousands, some new laid, some
hatching, while the fluttering young birds but just out of the
shell were under our feet where ever we walked. The island
was, perhaps, half a mile in diameter, and after satisfying our
curiosity by a thorough inspection of it we again embarked

to visit a much larger island two miles distant.

This one was about two and a half miles long and two miles wide, and showed unmistakable evidence of having been the crater of some long extinct volcano. It was a mass of rugged, irregular lava, with occasional coves and flats of alkali dust. A more desolate spot can not be conceived. In coasting about the island we discovered off the western shore some boiling subaqueous springs, making the lake water so hot as to scald the hand thrust into it.[10]

For Bayley, the passage of three years between his experience and his writing about it did not dim in his memory the dangers or the details of the way he met them:

About two in the afternoon we started to return to Sammon's. We had got but a mile or two when a sudden squall broke over the lake from the west, quickly churning its surface into formidable waves that placed us in constant jeopardy. The boat was a leaky tub, and one man was kept busy bailing out the water that came through the seams as well as over the sides of the wretched craft. It was decided after a hasty consultation that it would be folly to attempt to reach shore in such a gale, and that our only safety lay in returning to the island. We did so, but came within a hair's breadth of going to the bottom several times before reaching terra firma.

The gale continued to increase from hour to hour all the afternoon, and not till nine P.M. did the wind die down. Meantime we wandered about the desolate island like shipwrecked mariners, sinking to our knees at every step on the fine, flour-like alkali. Not a drop of fresh water was to be found and we were perishing with thirst. To think of passing the night in such a place was too horrible, and at ten o'clock a majority of the company gained the reluctant consent of the rest to reembark for a second attempt to reach the shore.

The differences between what Muir remembered and what Bayley remembered in no way reduced the suspense each reported. But Bayley recounted more of the thinking and acting that led to saving their lives:

> It was desperate folly as we soon found, for although the
> wind had subsided the waves were still high, and tossed our
> frail boat mercilessly about. M. [Muir] sat in the bow to break
> off the waves with his broad back, and kept them from swamp-
> ing the boat. B. [Buckskin Bill] plied the bailer with unre-
> mitting zeal. C. [Charles Washburn] and myself pulled faith-
> fully at the oars, while Sammon managed the rudder. It was
> bright moonlight, so we could see to steer for the nearest
> shore. We had got about half way when a sudden gust ca-
> reened the boat so that she half filled with water. We all
> thought our last hour had come. I slipped off my boots and
> observed that M. had silently done the same, expecting that
> in case the boat sank we might possibly swim to shore. It was
> a vain hope for in that intensely alkaline water it would have
> been an impossibility to survive. We should have been eaten
> up and boiled alive even had we managed to float. Luckily,
> providentially, we were not forced to this emergency.
> Quick work with the bailer kept the staggering craft afloat
> until suddenly we glided into smooth water, where the waves
> had subsided and all was still. "Is this a miracle?" I asked.
> "Providence," said M., quietly.

Perhaps the work of "Providence" explained enough for
Muir, but Bayley's curiosity led him to question and find other
answers:

> We found on investigating the matter next day that we
> must have encountered the narrow current of Rush Creek
> where it sets strongly into the lake, producing a counter-
> influence to the surface agitation. At all events we had no
> further trouble in reaching shore, and at half-past two o'clock
> in the morning, with thankful hearts, again set foot on dry
> land. We were several miles from our starting point, but we
> were safe, and felt that we had been delivered from the very
> jaws of hell. Our joy knew no bounds.
> We cared not where we were to sleep, but, encountering a

little, filthy cabin, threw ourselves on the floor and slept
soundly till morning, awaking with the startling discovery
that we were in a den of hissing rattlesnakes that were gliding
about the room. Fortunately none of the party were bitten
and we escaped all dangers to reach home alive and well.

Were they snakes or were they rats? Muir restricted his published reporting of the rest of the Mono Lake experience to
descriptions of geologic and botanical wonders. He concluded
his story of the trip by mentioning the return of his party to
Yosemite Valley "by the old glacial pathway of Bloody Canyon."

George Bayley, neither daunted nor discouraged by the exi-
gencies of ill fortune, continued to relish every "delicious after-
taste" and to look for other samplings of "the spice of danger."

NOTES

1. William Frederic Bade, *The Life and Letters of John Muir* (Boston
and New York: Houghton Mifflin, 1924), Vol. I, p. 179.

2. Bade, *The Life and Letters of John Muir*, Vol. I, p. 201.

3. John Muir, "The Kings River Valley," *Daily Evening Bulletin* (San
Francisco) , August 13, 1875.

4. John Muir, "Mount Whitney," *Daily Evening Bulletin* (San Francisco) , August 24, 1875.

5. John Muir, "Summering in the Sierra," *Daily Evening Bulletin* (San
Francisco) , September 15, 1875.

6. George B. Bayley, "Mount Takhoma," *Overland Monthly,* VIII (September 1886) , p. 28.

7. Erwin G. Guddle, *California Place Names: A Geographical Dictionary*
(Berkeley and Los Angeles, Calif.: University of California Press, 1949),
p. 207.

8. Linnie Marsh Wolfe, ed., *John of the Mountains, The Unpublished
Journals of John Muir* (Boston: Houghton Mifflin, 1938) , p. 158.

9. Wolfe, *John of the Mountains,* pp. 205–7.

10. George B. Bayley, "Eleven Days in the High Sierra," *Stockton Daily
Independent* (Stockton, California) , December 21, 1878.

CHAPTER SEVEN

Or Even Shorter

BAYLEY HAD BECOME a true mountaineer. Nine successive sum-
mers in and about Yosemite had taught the war-whooping
banker the exacting art of rock climbing and the skill of tra-
versing slippery glaciers. He had developed the endurance required for long hours of effort at high altitudes. He would need
these attributes—plus a strong dose of Yankee pluck and luck—
when, in the next three years, he would twice achieve another
inaccessible pinnacle above the Yosemite Valley and in the following two decades twice challenge mighty Rainier.

Encouraged by his own successes and by Muir's admiration,
Bayley soon would reach the apex of another Yosemite pinnacle—the top of Mount Starr King. This climb, a first that put
George Bayley's name on the record but for which he asked no
public acclaim, won Muir's respect for Bayley's mountaineering
accomplishments.

Muir sent off his tribute to the San Francisco *Daily Evening
Bulletin.* In an article scorning newer travelers and warning
that unsuitable visitors were desecrating the Yosemite, he wrote:

>   As civilization rolls Yosemiteward there is a marked falling
> off in the quality of tourists. The first comers endured what
> to them were real dangers and hardships for the very love of
> wild nature alone, passing nights beneath the forest trees or
> rude cabin roofs, fording unbridged torrents and riding over
> rugged trails, to worship in the grandest of mountain temples,

or at least to seek adventures in a spirit that always predicates something higher. Now the mere doing of Yosemite is becoming the regular thing with all sight-seeing lovers of perpetual motion.

To listen to their conversation here, mere scrubby bits of wayside gossip, one could not infer there was a flower, a pine tree, or mountain within a thousand miles, always however with refreshing exceptions.[1]

It was here that Muir included his admiring description of his frequent companion:

A firm, condensed, muscular little man of my acquaintance comes aclimbing in the mountains every year. His love of alpine exercise seems to suffer no abatement, notwithstanding he scrambles most of the year among the dangerous heights and hollows of the San Francisco stock market and among the arithmetical banks and braes of banking. He is a short man, or even shorter, who disdaining the plush lawns and gravelly margins of Yosemite, pushes bravely out among the precipices of the loftiest Alps; scaling cliffs for the dear love of the danger, glissading adown glacier declivities and floundering through snow fountains with indomitable perseverance, yet without any of the distinctive characteristics of the cautious mountaineer.

Mounts Shasta, Whitney, Lyell, Dana and the Obelisk, all have felt his foot; and years ago he made desperate efforts to ascend the South Dome [Half Dome], eager for the first honors, and certainly no one could be better qualified to succeed in a chance way; for with the grip and audacity of a squirrel, his tense muscular limb bundles ply with a pattering, twinkling motion, seemingly independent of ordinary holds.

Acceding to Bayley's request for no publicity, Muir referred to Bayley as Mr. Short:

The only kind of mountain climbing at which he appears

at a disadvantage are flood and earthquake taluses. The various blocks and bowlders of which they are composed are all placed by natural laws in exquisite rhythmical order, and the tuned mountaineer, bounding adown their curves, finds himself playing upon a grand instrument. But here Mr. Short finds difficulty and discord in pattering from key to key, like a lady with stumpy, abbreviated fingers, playing a piano. Upon plain flowing folds of granite, however, the case is different, and happily our hero has at length found what he long has sought—an accessible mountain, with name and fame deemed inaccessible, and that mountain is Starr King, the loftiest and most symmetrical of the Yosemite Domes.

Returning the other day from an extended excursion into the high Sierra, he determined an attempt upon it from the north, and now the silk handkerchief of a brave young lawyer who accompanied him, floats above it on the breeze, proclaiming the small fact, that with the exception of a few branches of spirey needles, the last of Yosemite inaccessibles has been conquested. To Anderson belongs the honor of first standing in the blue ether above Tissiack; and to the dauntless San Francisco Short belongs the first footprint on the crown of Starr King.

That first Starr King victory was in 1875. Two years later George Bayley reached the top again with another companion, one James D. Schuyler. Tipping the scales at 250 pounds,[2] Schuyler was an editor of the *Stockton Daily Independent*.[3] In a series of articles in his paper Schuyler described his stay in the valley in 1877. He told first of a dramatic climb with Bayley to the top of the Upper Yosemite Falls and next reported their historic ascent of Mount Starr King. In the first article Schuyler recounted the pull and temptation that the tops of the two falls exerted upon him, his first meeting the Bayleys, the challenges of endurance George posed, and the drama of climbing to the very top of the upper falls:

It had been a part of my plan to visit the foot of the upper fall, to which a good horse trail has been built, but I had not

thought it possible to scale the cliff to its summit and look
down upon the fall from the top where its vast height may be
better appreciated. Fortunately I had the previous day acci-
dentally made the acquaintance of a gentleman from San
Francisco, an attaché of the Bank of Nevada, who for twelve
years past has every summer taken a month's recreation in
and about the Yo Semite valley, and has acquired such a passion for mountain climbing that he has scaled not only every
height about Yo Semite, but has made the ascent of the principal peaks of the Sierra summit range, a part of the time in
company with Mr. John Muir, the geologist, with whom he
also visited the almost inaccessible Hetch-Hetchi valley. His
charming wife is equally fond of the exercise and accompanies
him on all his excursions. With some Oakland friends they
occupied a cottage attached to the hotel, and I found them all
cultured people and very delightful acquaintances. . . . They
had planned to ride to the foot of the upper Yo Semite Fall
and kindly invited me to join them, an invitation which I
gratefully accepted.

It requires a ride of four miles to reach the bottom of the
upper fall. As in this four miles an elevation of over 1,000
feet is attained the trail is quite steep but easily surmounted
by the valley saddle animals accustomed to such climbing.
The day's work not being a long one we did not get a very
early start and it was eleven o'clock before we reached the foot
of the fall. . . .

To reach the top of the fall from here required a rough
climb of at least 2,000 feet in perpendicular elevation without
the shadow of a trail. . . . I accepted Mr. Bayley's challenge to
accompany him to the top. Throwing off all superfluous
clothing, tying up our lunch in a handkerchief, and leaving
the ladies to return to the valley at their leisure, we started on
the ascent. The way led up a steep, narrow canyon over an
ancient rock avalanche overgrown with stiff chaparral.

Two hours of hard work brought us to the top of the mountain, when we descended to the very edge of the fall, with
what I considered to be very perilous work, but what my more
agile companion treated as mere child's play. We found our

friends waiting below for our appearance and we exchanged
signals with them. They were barely discernible to the naked
eye, their white handkerchiefs serving to give them a semblance of identity as human beings.[4]

As he had on the trip up Whitney, ebullient George again
pushed a boulder over the cliff:

> Some large boulders were nicely poised on the edge, which
> with a little exertion, we succeeded in throwing over. One of
> them weighed fully half a ton, and the effect as it went whiz-
> zing through the air over the giddy precipice was terrific. It
> seemed an endless time before it finally struck the bottom of
> the abyss and shivered into a thousand fragments, awakening
> the echoes with a sound equal to the discharge of a battery
> of artillery.
> Clambering up again from the narrow ledge upon which
> we had been poised 'twixt earth and sky, we ascended the
> stream a few hundred yards, crossed to the east side, and
> stripping off our clothes took a bath in a crystal, granite-
> lined pool.

The risks and frights appeared again on the descent:

> Our route homeward was over the mountain to the head of
> Indian Canyon and down that rugged stream to the Valley.
> Before starting we again descended to the brink of the fall on
> the opposite side from our other point of vantage, to get an-
> other peep into the yawning chasm. Creeping out upon an
> overhanging ledge of loose rocks that looked as though a
> slight earthquake would send them toppling to the bottom of
> the cliff, we looked over, holding nervously to the crannies in
> the rock. Even my companion afterwards confessed that he
> had there felt the first sense of giddiness he had experienced
> for years.

They reached the hotel at dark, rested the next day, which
was Sunday, and set out for Starr King on Monday. Schuyler

wrote vividly of the drama and glories of the climb, of the confidence George imparted, and of the paradox of fear combined with fun that George inspired:

> Two years ago the mountain was first ascended by George B. Bayley, Esq., of San Francisco, who took with him his Mexican guide and a Mr. Smith of San Francisco. Mr. Bayley having made arrangements to make a second ascent with his wife and a lady friend, I was invited to become one of the party.
> Knowing that we should be obliged to stop all night at the Glacier Point house, and that there were no sleeping accommodations for us there, we strapped a pile of blankets on behind our saddles and started off.... The steady up hill climb of four miles by trail to the Glacier Point House is a long one, but the superb views of the *bijou* valley below us served to beguile away the time and attract our constant attention, whiie we gave vent to the exuberance of our spirits in jolly conversation, laughter and song.[5]

From Glacier Point they went on:

> We were not long in reaching a point where we were obliged to leave our horses and proceed the remaining distance on foot. A climb of perhaps half a mile over broken debris brought us to the "saddle," a point which even the ladies had no difficulty in reaching by a slow but sure process of putting one foot before the other. But here began the serious part of the work.... The ladies openly avowed that they would not budge an inch beyond where they were, a resolve for which I cannot too warmly commend their judgment.

Mr. Schuyler found the demands better met by one of Bayley's dimensions than by one of his own:

> We had brought with us a stout rope about fifty feet in length, and taking one end of this in his teeth Mr. Bayley started up the slope. His boots were provided with hobnails and by their aid and the exercise of that remarkable agility

Map showing the route taken by George B. Bayley and James D. Schuyler on their climb to the peak of Mount Starr King in 1877. Two years earlier Bayley was the first person to conquer what John Muir called "the loftiest and most symmetrical of the Yosemite Domes." (Map by James A. Bier)

with which he is peculiarly gifted, he scrambled up the length of the rope until he stood on a narrow ledge some three inches wide running across the face of the mountain. Here he took a turn of the rope around his wrist and bracing himself back against the rock called to me to follow. I protested that I could not, that it was useless to imperil our lives in attempting to go on. He answered reassuringly and begged me to try it. I therefore thought I would go as high as he was standing and then persuade him to return. Putting my weight on the rope to test his power to hold me, I found it pretty firm and started up. He is a small man but very muscular, and I trusted in him implicitly. I found I got up easier than I expected, and as he started off for another ascent I could not demur too strongly, especially as he assured me that the hard climbing would be over after the next 100 feet. Leaving me standing on the ledge, he walked along it to the face of a low wall, in the corner of which he scrambled up to another good footing point about fifty feet further. The rope had slipped from my grasp, and when he threw the end out toward me it would not reach. Fortunately he had a small piece of baling rope in his pocket with which he spliced out the longer one so that I could grab it. As I had not dared to follow along the narrow, contracting ledge to a point directly beneath him, my next climb was necessarily in a diagonal direction. This was not pleasant, as after the first step or two my feet slipped from under me and I rolled and slid over to the wall, clinging to the rope for dear life. If it had broken I should have quickly met a terrible fate. My companion laughed heartily at my mishap to give me assurance, but my knees were barked and I was considerably bruised. I got up all right, however, and my companion started on. Going about twenty feet he braced himself again and told me he had a firm footing, so I again walked up the rope to where he was. I was at a loss to find the footing, however, and it was with the greatest difficulty I managed to twist one foot into a crevice and cling to a half inch ledge with my finger nails. How he had managed to hold himself in position against the strain of my weight, which is not light, I could not conceive.

Mount Starr King, another Yosemite peak George B. Bayley was the first to climb. (Photo courtesy U.S. National Park Service)

"We are in for it now, Schuyler," said he. "Stick here and be ready to catch me if I should fall."

"In for it! I should say we were," I replied. "If you come down, do it as easy as you can. I can't hold on here very long."

Up he went again, but as he had anticipated, he had not gone more than ten feet before he came sliding down, bringing up on my shoulders, his boot heels cutting furrows in my hands and starting the blood. Three times this was repeated.

Here a knife saved them from destruction:

At last I exclaimed, "See here, Bayley, this thing is getting monotonous. We'll go to the bottom in short order if you do that again. For God's sake give me your knife!"

Taking the strong, curved back of the knife used for relieving dirt from horses hoofs, I applied it as a lever to a thin slab of rock which I succeeded in breaking out. This left a nice little ledge nearly two inches deep into which I threw my knee and breathed a sigh of relief. Mr. Bayley then took the knife and pried out a loose slab about ten feet long and an inch thick, lying on edge in the angle of the wall. The footing of the slab was not disturbed, but the top being pulled out four or five inches it served as a ladder for Mr. Bayley to climb over the slippery place that had given him several falls, and gave me something to cling to.

After that we got along without further trouble, by a repetition of our experience below, and a couple of hundred feet brought us to easy walking, when we quickly mounted to the top. . . . We planted our flag in a conspicuous place, and after I had recovered my equanimity, started on the descent. The ladies, who had been nervously watching our climb from below, hearing every word of our conversation and expecting every moment to see us dashed to the bottom, gave us an encouraging cheer to which we heartily responded.

We came down easily, without mishap, until we reached the diagonal descent, which I was obliged to make, when I slipped again, sliding down the full length of the rope, and fetching up with my toes in a friendly ledge. This fall was more serious than the one received when we went up, as I came very near pulling my companion out of his position. As it was he afterwards exhibited a black and blue mark encircling his arm where the rope had cut into the flesh. . . .

At four o'clock we reached our animals, and before dark had got back to the Glacier Point House, where we enjoyed a good supper, eaten with uproarious hilarity. . . . We did not sleep much, as Mr. Bayley was haunted with a remarkable and contagious fund of animal spirits and kept the house in an uproar until 2 o'clock in the morning.

NOTES

1. John Muir, "Summering in the Sierra," *Daily Evening Bulletin* (San Francisco) , August 26, 1876.

2. *Grand Register of the Cosmopolitan*, in the Yosemite Museum, June 20, 1877.

3. *Stockton Directory, 1876.*

4. James D. Schuyler, "Mountaineering about Yosemite," *Stockton Daily Independent*, Vol. XXXII, No. 136, July 11, 1877, p. 3.

5. James D. Schuyler, "The Ascent of Mount Starr King," *Stockton Daily Independent*, Vol. XXXII, No. 137, July 12, 1877, p. 3.

CHAPTER EIGHT

Eleven Days in the High Sierra

INDEED GEORGE BAYLEY had become a top-notch mountaineer. His active curiosity, keen observation, and continued association with John Muir spurred Bayley to acquire more and more mountaineering technique. His growing knowledge expanded to include the experience of Bayley the naturalist and Bayley the geologist. He continued to go to the Yosemite every summer and pack into the back country.

In 1878 he joined the growing list of writers—Whitney, King, Hutchings, and Muir—who were disseminating reports of the grandeur of the mountains. Bayley published that year in his friend Schuyler's *Stockton Daily Independent* and simultaneously in the San Francisco *Argonaut,* a young weekly of national literary status, a journal of a summer trip on horseback through what is now a part of the John Muir Trail.[1] Bayley was accompanied by Mrs. Bayley, a Mrs. Georgia Smith, a Mrs. Tabor, Charles E. Peregoy of Mariposa as cook, and Manuel Flores as guide. The expedition carried them through some of the most stupendously beautiful—then virtually unknown—country in the world. Entitled simply "Eleven Days in the High Sierra," the day-by-day account began:

Grand and beautiful as are the scenes of that incomparable spot of earth, Yosemite Valley, the tourist who contents himself with a sight of its majestic walls and peerless cataracts little realizes how much of the picturesque in nature he might have enjoyed within a short ride of its perimeter. The beaten paths of tourist travel are trodden by thousands, but to the adventurous few who depart therefrom is reserved the enjoyment of new undescribed wonders. I believe there are very few who know anything about the region lying to the eastward of the Valley, or deem it worthy of a visit. For the benefit of the traveling public I propose narrating some of the incidents of an eleven days' horseback ride through the elevated, rugged region that forms the backbone of the State, expanding the notes of a hastily kept diary.

The party was five, three ladies and two gentlemen, all of San Francisco, with Manuel Flores for guide—the best and about the only intelligent guide for the region about and beyond Yosemite—and Chas. E. Peregoy of Mariposa, former proprietor of the Mountain View House between Yosemite and Clark's presiding over the indispensable culinary department. I mention their names for they have few equals in their specialties, and I can recommend them most heartily to any inclined to follow in our footsteps.

We started from Yosemite June 24th, at 10 A.M. climbing the southern wall by the torturous trail to Glacier Point, our outfit consisting of blankets (three pairs for each person), a light tent for shelter, and the necessary "grub," cooking utensils, etc., condensed into two packs of about one hundred and eighty pounds each. From the Glacier Point House we struck off to the southward, passing between Mount Starr King and Sentinel Dome, crossing the Bridal Veil Creek, and leaving the Valley of the Illillouette to the left. Our first camp was at Dead Horse Meadows—an unattractive name, but a beautiful spot, and what was of more importance, having plenty of feed for the mules.

Tuesday, June 25. Broke camp at 7:30 o'clock traveling a little east of south and skirting the flanks of Buena Vista Peak. The route lay through the virgin forest, untouched by the axe of man. Enormous sugar pines and firs towered rank on rank along the mountain sides, an unbroken phalanx of giants for miles. By noon we had reached the shores of Crescent Lake, twenty miles from Yosemite, and near the boundary line between Mariposa and Fresno counties. The lake is in the exact form of a crescent, with both horns pointing westward. Its shores are densely wooded on three sides and on the fourth towers a vertical cliff of rock, from which one may look down a long gateway in the hills and see the San Joaquin plains in the dim perspective. The water of the lake is clear as crystal and very deep.

On its border is a log cabin inhabited in summer by a mighty Nimrod, Jim Duncan, who has killed forty or fifty bears within the past six years of his occupancy of the cabin. The country abounds in game, deer, cinnamon bear, an occasional grizzly, and smaller game *ad infinitum*. It is due east from Clark's, from which it can be reached in a distance of twenty miles—an easy half day's ride. Leaving this delightful spot we continued our route, visiting Lost Lake, an emerald gem set in the hills with such care that it requires an expert to find it. At half past two we crossed the south fork of the Merced, descending into and climbing out of a deep narrow canyon, and by five o'clock had reached our second camping place, a large tributary of the San Joaquin. In this day's ride we had crossed the divide between the headwaters of the Merced and San Joaquin, and completely turned the western flanks of the obelisk group of peaks, of which Mount Clark, Red, Gray, and Black Mountains are the most prominent.

So spoke Bayley the naturalist. Then he became climber again. He reported the shifting from one role to the other:

The entrance to the Chiquito Meadows is very rugged. Riding was impossible. We could only pick our way, leading our straggling animals over debris of ancient glaciers. Rugged though it be, it is the only possible way to pass from Crescent Lake to the Chiquito Meadows. Once at this lofty resting place, our animals enjoyed an abundance of grass and were rested from their painful journey.

Wednesday, June 26. Continuing a southeasterly course we traveled over an easy rolling country, reaching the Jackass Meadows at noon. These remarkable meadow lands lie at the

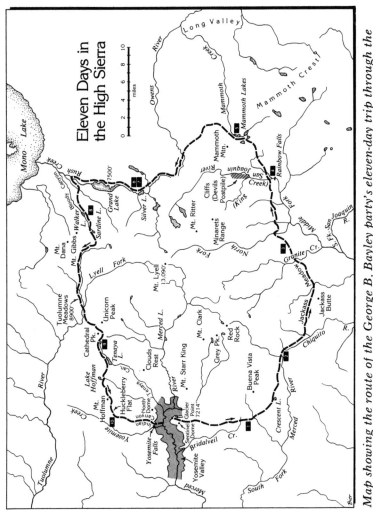

Map showing the route of the George B. Bayley party's eleven-day trip through the back country of Yosemite. (Map by James A. Bier)

foot of Black Mountain, forty miles from Yosemite, or about twenty-two due southeast as the crow flies. They are four or five miles long and intersected by long tongues of tamarack and pine timber that divide the meadows into a succession of grassy parks fringed with trees. Here we found hundreds of horses and the first band of sheep encountered on the trip. We traveled through them for several miles and then struck off due east, reaching Granite Creek, a tributary of the San Joaquin, at three o'clock. This stream is very wide, deep and swift, and the horses were obliged to swim. The passage was made in safety, however, although our packs were slightly wet. We made camp at four o'clock in some beautiful meadows on a mountain side overlooking the north fork of the San Joaquin, where feed was plenty. We began to be sensible that we had reached a great altitude, as the nights were extremely cold, and the ice formed on the borders of the streams.

Thursday, June 27. We were on our way early, and after riding a few hours met three of the most villainous looking fellows that ever assumed human shape. We surprised them eating breakfast and imagined we had fallen into a bandits' encampment. One of them who was minus an eye, and flourished a huge knife in his hand, looked as though he would cut a throat with as much *sang froid* as the haunch of venison he was slicing. It was questionable, however, which party was the most surprised. They told us they had been sent out by sheep men to put the trail in order, and as we afterwards found indications of their work we could not disbelieve them, but the ladies experienced a sense of relief when they were no longer visible.

About one hour after leaving them we crossed the north fork of the San Joaquin, a stream which is here 120 feet wide and 15 to 20 feet deep, swift and clear, fresh from the snow banks encircling Mount Ritter some fifteen miles away. A huge tree that must have been two hundred feet high when growing on the bank had been felled across the stream, its upper surface smoothed off with the axe and rough railings placed on the sides, forming a very secure bridge, barely wide enough for a horse to pass over. We had been steadily ascend-

ing until we were getting into the region of almost perpetual
snow, and at twelve o'clock halted for our lunch on a vast
snow bank where our last bottle of cocktails was drunk, cooled
deliciously by the crisp crystal of congealed vapor.

Bayley had his many facets. Besides mountaineer, geologist,
and naturalist, he was daredevil, aesthete, sensualist, and artist.
The facets could be separate; they could merge. The mountaineer's eye could blend with the eye of the artist and did:

> The whole country was covered with snow. The solitude
> was unbroken by the sound of bird or beast. No footprints
> were visible. We were alone with nature amid the deep hush
> that pervades her in her grander forms. At two o'clock we
> reached the summit of the San Joaquin pass 9,500 feet above
> sea level, the lowest depression in the range in this section of
> the country, although not precisely in the dividing ridge
> between the waters of the Owens River and the San Joaquin.
> It was rather a sag in the spur of the Minarets. In ascending
> to the pass we rode over miles of snow, sometimes crossing a
> summer rivulet on a bridge of snow and anon tramping
> through the slush and ice that filled all the hollows and mead-
> ows of the heights. Drifts of snow from fifteen to thirty feet
> deep lay on both sides of the pass, a most fortunate circum-
> stance for us, as the way was so rugged that even with the
> snow to aid us it was well nigh impassable.
>   You will ask what was the view from the summit: My pen
> is incapable of picturing its grandeur. Mount Ritter and the
> Minarets lay directly before us, rising up from their pinnacles
> and towers, so steep that even the snow could not cling to
> them, but lay piled in masses at their feet. Nearer than these
> was a lesser peak over whose summit a combing snow drift
> seemed to hang like a frozen wave suspended in mid air, and
> reflecting tints that would have inspired the pencil of Brad-
> ford as no arctic iceberg could have done. Behind us, away
> beyond, over the snow fields, the broken country we had
> passed mellowed by its mantle of forest and leveled by the
> smoothing-iron of distance perspective, stretched away as far

as we could see in a billowy landscape.

In an hour and a half we had picked our way through the pass and descended to a stream called by our guide Warren Creek (probably erroneously, as I think Warren Creek proper is further north), a tributary of the San Joaquin that rises in the Minarets and goes brawling down a narrow valley over a rocky channel, like "Iser, rolling rapidly." We found the water ten or twelve feet deep, sixty feet wide, very swift and icy cold. Another rustic bridge of two parallel logs had been made by sheepmen here, but it was too insecure to bear our animals and we were obliged to unpack, "tote" our "plunder" across on foot, while Manuel and I swam the horses over.

We camped on this creek, about three miles below the bridge, and half a mile above its junction with the middle fork of the San Joaquin. The camp was in the loveliest spot that human fancy can conceive. I cannot describe it, but will ask you to imagine a rich grassy meadow interspersed with fine evergreen trees, a foaming cascade tumbling over rounded and polished granite boulders in "the way the water comes down at Lodore," a tall, somber volcanic cliff, somewhat resembling the Palisades of the Hudson, rising in perpendicular height 2,000 feet above the meadow at its feet; mix up a good deal of moonlight and starlight with it all, and you have the principal ingredients of a scene which kept us at the camp fire till after midnight absorbed in its beauty.

The next day their guide led them to the discovery of what is now called Rainbow Falls. Bayley described it and illustrated his article in both newspapers with a cut from a drawing of the falls by his friend, the artist William Keith. In publishing the article in the *Stockton Daily Independent*, the editor commented that to his knowledge these as yet unnamed falls had never before been described:

Friday, June 28. The incidents of this day were to be the climax of all we had yet passed in point of interest and enjoyment. Manuel Flores, our sagacious guide, who had brought us thus far safely over trackless wilderness without the shadow of a trail, had told us that two years before, near this spot as he thought, while traveling from Long Valley to Clark's he had lost his way and found a number of blazes on the trees that led to the brink of a cliff from which he had caught a glimpse through the forest of a peaceful waterfall, rivaling those of Yosemite. The blazes had doubtless been made by the hunters who were lost like himself. At the intimation of scenery of this kind in the vicinity we at once resolved to search for it.

We left our camp on foot, and descended to the mouth of the creek, half a mile. Here it joins the middle fork of the San Joaquin river, which is at this point a stream as large as the Merced in Yosemite, although so short a distance from its source. Ascending this stream a quarter of a mile we found we were obliged to leave its bed and climb up the wall on the northern side about two hundred feet to a terrace overlooking the river. We had not gone far before some one shouted, "See the spray." A dense cloud of mist appeared, a roar of descending water was borne on the wind, and a sudden turn confronted us with the falls.

The view we had of them from our standpoint was entrancing; on the north side a bold dyke of bare volcanic rock, on a shelf of which we were standing, seemingly thrust up through the crust of the earth, half a mile high, scarred and seamed with narrow crevices down which we could rattle thin stones that must have descended hundreds of feet before reaching bottom; on the south a sloping mountain covered with trees; before us the whole river made a vertical leap from over a ledge as square cut as a stone mason could make it, descending into a deep pool that was perfectly inaccessible, and having as a background to complete the picture the snow capped peak whose wondrous tints had captivated our senses all the day previous. We estimated the falls to be three hundred feet high, an estimate which is rather under than over the mark. The stream is from eighty to one hundred feet in width at the brink. It impresses one with a sense of beauty, grandeur, and power quite as deeply as the Vernal Falls of Yosemite.

Manuel and myself succeeded in clambering down to the very brink of the falls, where we could look into the chasm below. Above the falls the river glides over the smooth bed of flaky slate, and seemed totally devoid of the fruits of attrition—sand, gravel, or mud.

These remarkable falls are almost unknown to the world. Much as I have climbed through the Sierra for many years past, I never before heard of them. They have never been described to my knowledge, and as they are off the natural lines of travel which those whose pursuits take them through this section would be apt to take, it is possible that we were the first to visit and appreciate them.

After enjoying this wild scene to our satisfaction we returned to camp, and at nine o'clock were again on our way. Passing over a low divide we descended to the middle fork of the San Joaquin, a few miles above the falls, and crossed on a log that had been felled and prepared as a sheep bridge. A few miles further and we were at the summit of the Sierra Nevada. So easy was the ascent, however, that we scarcely realized it, and were at a loss to know just where the waters parted. But when the view of Long Valley stretching away in dimness like an emerald ocean, burst upon us, we comprehended that we were descending into Owens River basin on the east side of that range.

Distance lent such enchantment to the sage brush plain that we almost thought we were getting into Paradise. Beyond the valley we have a view of the Inyo range for one hundred and fifty miles, overtopped by the White Mountain peak, which is said, by the Inyo people, to be the highest mountain in North America.

At twelve o'clock, after a very abrupt descent we came upon Mammoth Lake, a handsome sheet of water two miles long and a mile or more in width, set down deeply in the hills and surrounded with peaks ten thousand feet high, their summits covered with snow and their sloping sides clothed in forests of yellow pine, cedar, and silver fir. This is the real source of the Owens River, which is, however, fed by a chain of silvery lakes half a dozen or more in number in the im-

Rainbow Falls, which George B. Bayley and his party came upon in their eleven-day trip in the high Sierra in the summer of 1878. (Photo courtesy U.S. National Park Service)

mediate vicinity.

Bayley commented on the changes he observed since his long trek with Muir three years earlier:

Three years ago I had spent a Summer vacation in traveling over this section on a visit to Mt. Whitney, to the southward, but saw no sign of habitation. Now, we suddenly found ourselves in the midst of a busy mining district, with some six hundred or seven hundred miners busily engaged in sinking shafts, running tunnels, putting up log huts and tents, etc. Some prospector discovered silver ore here a year ago, and the croppings proving rich, others were attracted to the spot, and the developments made give promise of the most flattering character. General George S. Dodge, of Oakland, is owner of the Mammoth mine, the largest of the district. The settlement is called Mammoth City and there is not a woman in it. The houses are of logs and canvas and make quite a showing for a town. A saw mill has recently been put in operation near by, furnishing lumber for the embryo city. The town is seventy miles from Independence, with which it is connected by a good wagon road, and over which all supplies are hauled from Mojave, on the Southern Pacific Railroad, over two hundred miles across the desert. It is also connected by road with Aurora and Carson City. Mammoth City, whose high sounding title gives it a positive advantage in the struggle for existence, is at an elevation of about seven thousand feet, sixty miles in air line from Aurora and thirty miles south of Mono Lake.

As we rode into it the people turned out in a body to receive us, and they seemed fairly bewildered with the distinction of a visit from real live ladies. In answer to the question as to whether they had any good mines about there, one of them quaintly remarked, "Mines? The richest damnedest mines in the country, stranger, don't you forget it."

Four miles below the town in the alkali plain are some interesting geysers and mud springs, where the water perpetually boils and hot mud sputters and fumes like so many pots of hot mush. The water is strongly mineral, sulphur and iron predominating. From the spring the water runs over the ground four hundred feet before it is sufficiently cooled for bathing. Here at four P.M., we halted for the night at a base of rock forty feet high, which was so perfect a representation of a skull that we named our camp Golgotha. A mile below is another geyser, where three years ago I saw a column of water spouting up to the height of thirty or forty feet.

Saturday, June 29. At nine o'clock resumed our line of march in a northward direction, riding for sixteen miles or more over country upon which the curse of Jehovah seems to rest. It is a long alkali plain, interspersed with low, desolate hills and ancient lake beds long since drained by the sun. It has evidently been the scene of violent volcanic action and disturbance of the earth's crust. There is a place near here where, in the middle of a forest, the trees have been killed by subterranean heat for a space half a mile in diameter. Eleven years ago this place was so hot it was impossible to camp or travel over it. In another place the land has sunken 100 feet for an area of a couple of hundred acres, the cleavage lines being abruptly vertical and the trees still growing at the bottom of the pit. Where the alkali plain surges up to the line of pine forest we came upon Grant's Lake, a superb sheet of water, two miles long and a mile wide, connecting by a short link of water with Silver Lake, in which the water was so warm that it was not possible to drink it with any degree of comfort. Here we concluded to camp, having an abundance of fresh water from tributary streams. Silver Lake is filled with myriads of a species of shellfish resembling shrimps or small lobsters, and which are considered by the Mono Indians as quite a luxury.

Sunday, June 30. Rush Creek is the largest stream of water that takes its source in Sierra snows, and flows eastwardly. It drains numerous lakes that nestle among the bolder spurs of the summit range, and goes tearing down the steep declivities with noisy murmur that is only hushed as it calms down into an occasional lakelet, spreading for itself a mirror with which to reflect its surroundings, and finding its way at last into that alkaline sea—Mono Lake. We discovered that we were near one of the most remarkable cascades in this stream and started out to spend the Sabbath in exploration of our surroundings.

To Bayley "exploration of our surroundings" meant climbing to the top of the waterfall:

> We rode to the foot of the cascades, three and one-half miles distant, and, leaving our horses, scrambled up to the top. The mountain face stood at an angle of more than forty-five degrees—indeed it was nearer sixty degrees—so that for about four hundred feet in the center the cascade is nearly vertical, gliding down a polished surface into a clear pool fringed with ferns and pines. The entire height of the cascades exceeds 1,000 feet.

This cascade no longer flows over the rock. A dammed lake swallowing the beauty of the falls now provides back-up water for the city of Los Angeles. From the top of the cascade they started to climb another "inaccessible" peak:

> Reaching the top, Manuel and I started to climb a high peak between our standpoint and Mount Ritter. It proved an exceedingly hazardous and difficult undertaking on account of the steepness of the slope and the treacherous uncertainty of the friable surface rocks that make up the dead volcano. Its altitude was about eleven thousand feet; and, once upon its summit, a more comprehensive view of the contour of the country was afforded than we had yet had. To the west, the one grand feature of the picture was the unapproachable Mount Ritter, "goring the sky with ragged horn"—the matchless monarch of the Sierra. We had, in our past week's journey, seen it from the west and the south; from the east we now saw it from base to pinnacled crest only ten miles away. South of it, in the chain of summits, was the Minarets, while directly north stood Mount Lyell, proud of the living glacier that poured down its side. Mono Lake lay far below us to the

north. We counted no less than thirty-one small lakes from
the summit of this peak, each from a quarter of a mile to two
miles in diameter, the greater number being simply enlarge-
ments of Rush Creek.

Monday, July 1. Broke camp at seven o'clock, following the
course of Rush Creek from the Cascades several miles to a
place where we could swim the creek, when we continued
down its western bank for three miles until it opened out into
a large lake. A short ride across country brought us to Joe
Bohler's ranch, the Mecca of all sagebrush travelers. Bohler
is a character worthy of study. A tall, athletic German, he
leads a lonely, frugal bachelor life in the hills, subsisting on
an anchorite diet of bread and water, with a hobby for "hy-
giene" (as though anybody could be ailing in that climate!),
raising hay on his scattered meadows for sale at the mining
settlements in the valley. He is the very soul of hospitality,
and indulged us in fresh milk to our hearts' content. Four
miles from Bohler's is Mono Lake, one of the most remarkable bodies of water on the continent.

Here in his journal Bayley recalled his hair-raising exploration of Mono Lake with John Muir. In an earlier part of this
book Bayley's account was presented where it fell in the se-
quence of events on the Mount Whitney expedition. After that
digression his journal continued:

From Bohler's we rode four miles to camp at the foot of
Bloody Canyon, on the shores of a lake a mile and a half long,
where we were furiously beset by the swarms of the most
courageous mosquitoes.

Tuesday, July 2. Left camp early, passing through Bloody
Canyon on our westward course, reaching the summit of
Mono Pass at 10:30 A.M. Bloody Canyon is very properly
named. It is studded with sharp, flinty rocks, that cut the
mules' feet and legs, so that no animal passes through it without leaving a bloody track. At the summit of Mono Pass we
could readily imagine that we had passed through the transi-
tion from summer to winter, as the wind blew a heavy gale

from the west, sweeping through the snow-clad pass with marrow-chilling force. Snow lay in enormous drifts everywhere about us, fixed in masses unmoved by the wind by the compacting influence of the summer sun.

The top of Mono Pass, which is 10,500 feet high, is marked by strange and unexpected natural curiosity. It is a little lake of that peculiar, rock-bound, fathomless type which the tourist through the higher Sierra so frequently encounters. Its waters are clear as crystal, and on a calm day must reflect on its bosom the image of Mount Dana, lying directly north, as well as Mount Gibbs, over a shoulder of which the trail passes. The lake is considered almost bottomless; no one pretends to know how deep it is, possibly because no one has come to it prepared for deep-sea soundings. It bears the name of Sardine Lake, from the fact that in 1863 or '4 a pack mule loaded with sardines made a fatal misstep from the trail and slipped into the lake never more to appear. Into this ice-cold and snow-bound lake, Muir and I had, three years before, taken an elegant "header" from a rock some fifteen feet high, scrambling out upon the snow of its margin, after a few strokes, fairly glowing with the delicious shock. Such a plunge is worth a hundred dusty miles of travel.

At half-past one o'clock we reined up our steeds at the famous Soda Springs, in the Tuolumne Meadows. As an agreeable beverage, the water of these springs is preferable to any springs in the State. It is highly charged with carbonic acid gas, which keeps it perpetually bubbling and boiling, as it pours up from nature's laboratory. We found a cabin at the springs, owned by a man named Lambert, who bottles the water and takes it to Yosemite Valley, where it is the only soda water in use. The Tuolumne Meadows, in which the soda springs are located, are seven or eight miles long, stretching in an unbroken, gently descending slope of grassy meadow from the base of Mount Dana westward to Courthouse Rock, the main Tuolumne River flowing through the centre.

Pursuing our course down these charming meadows we were confronted by two of the most beautiful crags in all the Sierra—Cathedral Peak and Unicorn Peak—both rising up out

of dense forests of silver fir, interspersed with the graceful
Williamson spruce.

Bayley saw those peaks and then without fanfare proceeded
to achieve another climbing first, the top of Unicorn Peak:

Unicorn Peak rears up a slender horn of rock, gradually
diminishing to a little point, on which there is barely room
for two persons to stand, as I have demonstrated by a somewhat arduous climb. The peak overhangs at its summit, and
altogether has a most striking and picturesque appearance.
Cathedral Peak is no less remarkable in outline, its summit
being divided into vertical shafts, pinnacles, and sculptured
spires supported by massive buttresses. It is forbidding in
appearance to the boldest mountaineer, but its stupendous
massiveness, combined with its airy, cathedral-like architec-
ture, convey to the observer a deep sense of sublimity and awe.
Between these two peaks, deeply hidden in the forest that
surrounds it, lies Echo Lake, the wild scenery of whose shores
demands a more skillful pen than mine to depict. We found a
charming camping place that night on the shores of Glacial
Lake, some miles further on, but our animals suffered from
the lack of feed, and although it was in the middle of summer,
a roaring fire and warm blankets were most acceptable and
essential to comfort. Glacial Lake—of which the artist Munger has painted a picture that does it justice—would delight
the scientific heart of the geologist looking for a support to
the glacial theory.

Munger was one of the artists whose paintings Bayley collected, and he owned one called "Glacial Lake."[2]

On one shore the bare granite has been polished and
striated by the erosive force of resistless rivers of ice firmly
holding their granite chisels. The glacier has even left its tools
still stranded on the shore—huge boulders borne from some
distant mountain. The forest bounds the lake on one side,
reaching a tongue of hardy pines down to the very edge of the

narrow outlet of the lake, that conveys its waters by an almost
vertical plunge of two thousand feet into Lake Teneya.

Wednesday, July 3. We were so near Yosemite again that
we might have returned in a half day's ride, but resolved to
spend another day in further exploration. Accordingly we
started out early in the morning, skirting the head of Teneya
Canon, and making directly for Mount Hoffman, in whose
wild ravines heads Yosemite Creek, that rushes thence in
rapid course to the terrible leap into the Yosemite, known to
all the world as Yosemite Falls. On the way we passed Courthouse Rock, a wondrous shaft of granite, whose sheer precipitous walls rising twenty-five hundred feet perpendicularly
above its base impress one even more deeply with awe and
majesty than the far famed South Dome of the Yosemite.

They came to a spot from which they could see many of Bayley's conquests:

At one o'clock we reached a point of interest for which we
were searching—Lake Hoffman, a very deep, intensely blue
sheet of ice-water set on the bosom of Mt. Hoffman, just at
timber line, jealously guarded by surrounding crags. Here we
did justice to Peregoy's luncheon, feasting our eyes as well
with the distant views of all the outlying domes, crags, peaks,
and forest slopes that surround Yosemite: Sentinel Dome,
South Dome, Cloud's Rest, Mts. Lyell and Dana, Cathedral
and Unicorn Peaks. Mt. Starr King, Mt. Clark, and all the
most striking landmarks about the valley were spread out as a
panorama before us. Lake Hoffman can be easily reached
from Yosemite in a day's ride over a fair trail, and is well
worth all the effort it may cost to reach it. We lingered here
an hour and a half before again turning our faces homeward,
camping that night at 4:30 P.M. at Huckleberry Flat, a mile
and a half from the head of Indian Canyon, a narrow precipitous gorge entering Yosemite from the north.

Thursday, July 4. Saddling up at a moderately early hour,
we rode leisurely to the rim of the northern wall of Yosemite

at the head of Indian Canon, followed the brink to the top of
Yosemite Falls, lunched on the edge of the precipice where
the stream takes its vertical plunge of 1,600 feet, then resumed
our course down the zigzag trail by the side of the fall, reaching the hotel from which we had started ten days before at
3:30 P.M.

Indian Canyon and the top of Yosemite Falls were familiar
territory to George from his honeymoon and from his first climb
with Mr. Schuyler.

We had swept around a circle whose centre I will place at
Mount Lyell for convenience (the common corner of Mariposa, Fresno, and Inyo Counties) , and whose periphery by the
winding and erratic course we traveled, measured some two
hundred odd miles. We got back without accident, the ladies
having endured the hardships and fatigue of the trip with
remarkable strength and courage. Such a trip is rarely taken
by ladies, and it may be well to remark that those of whom I
speak were not novices at mountain climbing, having ascended the heights and ridden the animals of Yosemite for
years past.

The geographical position of our route may be traced on
any map by the foregoing description, or it may be roughly
imagined when I say that within the boundaries of the circle
we had encompassed lie Mount Lyell, Mount Dana, Mount
Ritter, the Minarets, Mount Clark, Gray Mountain, Red
Mountain, Mount Starr King, Cloud's Rest, Cathedral Peak,
Unicorn Peak, and other lesser elevations.

Of all these mountain heights, Mount Ritter is the most
difficult and most dangerous to ascend, and it has been ascended by but four persons to my knowledge. Its crumbling
rocks and vertical pinnacles do not invite the cautious mountaineer to a trial of of his prowess.

That brief sentence is the only indication that Bayley might
have been among the few to have climbed to the summit of

Mount Ritter. He admitted to having achieved the tops of Mounts Dana and Lyell:

> Mount Dana, at whose feet we rode in crossing Mono Pass, is very easy of ascent, and may be reached in two day's ride from Yosemite. From its summit you look down upon Mono Lake nestling far below and resembling a wash basin. It is a laundryman's paradise, if Mark Twain's story be true, and a wash basin that would be a fortune if some philanthropic Titan would set it down in the heart of San Francisco. The elevation of Mount Dana is 13,227 feet. Mount Ritter is estimated at a little in excess of 13,250 feet. Mount Lyell is 13,200 feet, while Mono Lake is 6,500 feet. The Soda Springs lie at an elevation of 8,500 feet.
>
> I do not know that this narrative, for which my diary has given me the material, will incite any adventurous tourists to follow in our footsteps, but to travelers in this region I offer this gratuitous advice concerning their equipment: Nothing save what is absolutely needful should be taken, two or three changes of underclothing, plenty of blankets, and the necessary provisions and cooking utensils being all that is required, no tent even being wanted unless there are ladies in the party. Stout shoes or boots, with the soles well studded with nails are absolutely necessary for climbing, and a flannel shirt and the common blue overalls make the lightest and most serviceable mountain costume.

How different would be a list of necessities for the trip today, a hundred years later. When Bayley scaled all those rocks and peaks he used no pitons and no crampons, and when he camped he had no Coleman stove, no packaged rations, and no sleeping bag:

> I may here mention that the ladies of our party all rode astride, and in no other way would it have been possible for them to have traveled over the rough country we encountered. It is the common-sense way to ride in the mountains and is infinitely safer and less fatiguing, both for horse and rider. One other important point, be sure of the "doctor," i.e. your

cook, for upon him mainly depends the comfort and pleasure of the cruise, and it is astonishing what a variety of well-cooked and appetizing dishes are at the command of a good mountain cook. From Lake Tahoe on the north, to Mount Whitney, on the south, the whole range of the Sierra is one grand camping ground, and the whole extent of country between these two points, some three hundred miles, can be compassed in a summer's vacation.

In our own day, when the whole region is laced with trails intersecting the north-south trunkline called the John Muir Trail, when Yosemite Valley is fighting a smog problem, and a busy highway passes near the Tuolumne Meadows soda springs, it is not hard to feel nostalgia for the pristine wilderness Bayley knew. And one can read prophecy in his remark that "From Lake Tahoe on the north, to Mount Whitney, on the south, the whole range of the Sierra is one grand camping ground. . . ."
He finished with a bit of advice about mechanics:

I have always preferred making my early start from the Yosemite Valley, partly from desire to get a yearly view of it, but mainly because a good outfit can always be obtained there at reasonable expense, but any mountain town near the Sierra will do as well, and in the next year when the new road to the Yosemite via Fresno Flat, shall have been built, the tourist will be able to reach the San Joaquin Falls I have described in a day's easy riding from Fresno Flat over a fair trail, and can thence push on to Mammoth Lake, the Hot Springs and Geysers in five to six hours. From the middle of June to October, any of these trips can be made with safety and pleasure, the earlier month being best as feed for the animals becomes very scant in the wake of the sheep, the summer pest of the mountains. Our eleven days in the Sierra were all too short.[3]

In mind and body and experience George had been readied by the Yosemite and its "boy's play" for Mount Rainier, king of all the mountains.

N O T E S

1. George Bayley, "Eleven Days in the High Sierra," *Stockton Daily Independent* and San Francisco *Argonaut*, December 21, 1878; hereafter cited as Bayley, "Eleven Days. . . ."

2. Probate of the will of Gertrude K. Bayley, Oakland, Alameda County, 1917.

3. Bayley, "Eleven Days. . . ."

CHAPTER NINE

Chicken Bayley

SCRABBLING UP YOSEMITE'S pinnacles and sliding down its cliffs—
the "boy's play" that prepared George Bayley to conquer Rainier—occupied him only one out of the twelve months of each
year. The other eleven he devoted to bread-winning. He continued his daily commute to his job at the Bank of Nevada in
San Francisco with Gertrude driving the buggy to and from the
ferry. He spread his financial interests well beyond the confines
of the note-teller's cage. With his characteristic blend of sure-
footedness and daring and with the stock exchange within easy
walking distance of the bank, his buying and selling and specu-
lating in stocks gathered momentum.[1] His income grew to a size
that enabled him to pay life insurance premiums of four thousand dollars a year and to leave at his death in 1894 the largest
single insurance legacy that had ever been paid out in the history of California.[2] It was fitting that in the late eighties he
listed his occupation in the *Oakland Directory* as "capitalist."[3]

But it was not as a banker or investor, it was as a poultry
breeder that he attracted the most attention during that period.
On both sides of the bay and in the mountains he earned for
himself the sobriquet of "Chicken Bayley." The name was no
sarcastic pun on his physical courage. Not until well after the
turn of the century did "chicken" acquire the meaning that it
has today. In George's day it described him by naming what
most filled his mind and energy.

In the eighties he patented, promoted, and began the manufacture of the Pacific Incubator, invented by one John Peterson, who came to manage Bayley's Oakland Poultry Yard and live in a cottage on the property.[4] This invention prompted the poultry editor of the *Pacific Rural Press* to compare its lightening of the hen's labors with "amelioration of mankind" through "improved washing machines, churns, and cheese making apparatus."[5] In a full-page weekly ad for his yard and products in that same paper George could claim that the incubator was "in general use throughout the Pacific Coast, and is giving universal satisfaction."[6] Unsolicited letters to the editor in other issues bear out users' approval. When an early detractor, a Mr. Dias of Napa, drew Bayley into a debate, Chicken Bayley's lively defense showed both his down-to-earth Yankee practicality and his maverick spirit:

> Now, I claim that the Pacific, after a three years' trial, is a thorough success, turning out from 75% to 90%, and frequently as high as 95% of *healthy* and *strong* chicks from tested eggs. . . .
>
> Now, if Mr. Dias had any knowledge of the working of the Pacific Incubator and had not jumped at conclusions, he could (I hope) be readily made to understand why the thermometer in the water would not show the same temperature as would one laid upon the eggs or suspended directly over them; and it may be interesting to him, in this connection, to know that the doors of the machine are kept open for the last three or four days of incubation, and that there is a constant stream of fresh air at all times passing over the eggs.
>
> This is a vital point in artificial incubation, to which we are led by the action of the hen herself, who sometimes, for a half hour at a time, pushes the eggs away from herself to the edge of the nest.[7]

Here George Bayley managed the delicate process of temperature control by substituting a mechanical device for a mother. A little more than a year later, when he was to have no choice about fixing the degree of hot or cold, the same George Bayley was to freeze his toes and scald his fingers during a sleepless night in that wind-torn and steamy ice cavern near the summit of mighty Rainier. Soon after he accomplished that historic climb of 1883 and recovered from it, he swung back to poultry. He and thirteen other prominent fanciers—all interested in temperature control of incubators—organized the Pacific Poultry Association.[8] They planned a poultry fair to make the community more aware and knowledgeable about what was going on in the field.

At a meeting in San Francisco on November 5, 1883, the association chose Bayley to be its first president. At the first exhibit, the week before Christmas, among some eight hundred entrants in fifteen categories Bayley's birds won twelve first prizes plus the solid silver sweepstakes cup.[9] Those firsts were for his Light Brahmas, his Dark Brahmas, his Partridge Cochins, Buff Cochins, Bearded Silver Polish, Bearded Golden Polish, Golden Seabright Bantams, Wyandottes, Houdins, Plymouth Rocks, Golden Spangled Hamburgs, Silver Spangled Hamburgs, and several kinds of pigeons, including tumblers. The sweepstakes cup he won for the best exhibit of fowls was an elaborate trophy depicting the body of a woman crowned with elegant looking silver chickens.[10]

At about this time he quit his job at the Bank of Nevada, after nearly ten years, to devote his working months to poultry and to his life as an independent capitalist.[11] Re-elected president of the poultry association in 1885[12] and again in 1886,[13] he saw his poultry and his incubator continue to carry off prizes in shows at the California State Fair[14] and at the Mechanics Institute Fair of 1885.[15]

George Bayley was making a distinctive contribution to California's enormously expanding capacity to produce food. By 1885 the gigantic harvests of the Great Valley had made it the most productive wheat region in the world. San Franciscans owned and financed most of the ranches. Although the Comstock silver strike had collapsed five years earlier, new technologies now permitted industrial-age entrepreneurs of San Francisco to blast large quantities of gold ore from the deep, hardrock mines of the Sierra foothills. Amid continuing prosperity, San Francisco became more and more preoccupied with the pleasures of the good life—good eating in particular. The institution of the "free lunch" swelled to incredible dimensions, and restaurants and saloons vied for the choicest delicacies. Fancy poulterers—George Bayley's customers—were among those who sold the chickens, turkeys, and squabs to taverns, inns, hotels, and other gourmet eating establishments.

His fifty-page Oakland Poultry Yard catalog details the ways in which he acted as provider of necessities for every part of the poultry business.[16] Descriptions of their virtues and engravings depicting the elegance of thirty kinds of fowls—chickens, ducks, geese, turkeys, and pigeons—fill the first twenty-eight pages of the plump booklet. Then come details and testimonials about the Pacific Incubator. The brochure quotes a letter of enthusiastic praise from a patron in Los Angeles County:

> I feel it a duty to give you my testimony in favor of your incomparable Incubator. The simplicity of its construction places it far ahead of any machine that has ever been invented, in my opinion. A child can run it successfully. In my first trial I hatched nearly 90 per cent. of the fertile eggs. May success attend you.

A spontaneous letter from nearby Santa Clara County exemplifies the tone of all twenty letters that the pamphlet quotes:

> My first brood of chicks hatched out yesterday and the average was 80 per cent. of the fertile eggs. How is that for a novice and the Pacific Incubator.

Another supporter makes it clear that he told his friends about his successes:

> Over 85 per cent. has been my average this winter. Send me two of your 200-egg machines. I have sold them to neighbors. Your brooder a complete success. Haven't lost a chick so far.

Other pages depict and describe the glass house containing brooders for chicks that was used at the yard, as well as lists,

THE PACIFIC INCUBATOR,

(PATENTED JANUARY 30, 1883.)

MANUFACTURED BY GEO. B. BAYLEY, AT THE

OAKLAND POULTRY YARDS,

Corner Castro and Seventeenth Streets, Oakland, Cal.

Where they can be seen in Constant Operation.

Agents in New York: Messrs. Henderson & Stoubenborough, 270 Pearl Street.

			Boxed for Shipment.			
No. 0—Capacity	108 Eggs,		Weight, 100 lbs.	Price, $ 35.		Boxing, $1.00
No. 1—	"	216	" " 180 "	" 50.		" 1.50
No. 2—	"	324	" " 210 "	" 70.		" 2.00
No. 3—	"	420	" " 250 "	" 85.		" 2.50
No. 4—	"	600	" " 300 "	" 100.		" 2.50
No. 5—	"	800	" " 330 "	" 150.		" 3.00
No. 6—	"	1000	" " 375 "	" 180.		" 3.00

Any Special Size Required will be Manufactured to Order.

The above Cut represents the second size Incubator, (No. 1,) and will represent the larger sizes, with the addition of one or more drawers.

This machine is made of the best Galvanized Iron, and well-seasoned Sugar Pine, and the exterior case is finished to resemble a chest of drawers. With reasonable care it will last a life-time.

The dimensions of the various sizes are as follows : and they can be kept in any room in the house, being of a very ornamental appearance.

No. **0**, 36 inches high, 26 x 24 inches square.				No. **4**, 62 inches high, 31 x 29 inches square.		
No. **1**, 44 "	"	26 x 24 "		No. **5**, 62 "	35 x 34 "	
No. **2**, 51 "	"	26 x 24 "		No. **6**, 72 "	35 x 34 "	
No. **3**, 51 "	"	29 x 27 "				

George B. Bayley patented, promoted, and manufactured the Pacific Incubator at his Oakland Poultry Yards. (Photo courtesy California Historical Society Library)

BRONZE TURKEYS.

**First Premium on Pair at the California Poultry Association's Exhibit of 1885, and
Special, as the most valuable Fowls shown. SCORE 100 POINTS.
Weight of Gobbler 46½ pounds.**

The bronze Gobbler at maturity, reaching forty pounds and upwards, strutting in
full plumage in the early spring, is one of the finest sights of the farm-yard. This is one of
the largest and hardiest of all the breeds, and has been so long bred for size and plumage
that good birds well cared for can be relied upon to produce their own likeness in weight
and plumage. Gobblers at nine months old, or the beginning of the first breeding season,
frequently reach the weight of 25 to 28 lbs. and the hens 14 to 18 lbs. The second year
will add to the weight of the Gobblers 6 to 8 lbs., and to the Hens 4 or 5 lbs. A
few of the Gobblers will reach 40 lbs. the third year, and a few of the Hens 22. *Extreme
weights* are 45 lbs. for Gobblers, and 24 for Hens.

A bronze Gobbler running with ordinary Hen Turkeys will make a difference in a
brood of twelve young Turkeys of 5 pounds each ; that is, 60 pounds, worth, at 25 cts. per
pound, $15, besides a much greater percentage of the young reaching maturity, owing to
the extreme hardiness of this breed.

Eggs.. ....$7.00 per dozen.
Fowls (according to age) .... $20 to $30 per trio.
Young Gobblers.................................. ....$10 to $15 each.
A small number of 2 or 3-year-old Gobblers can be supplied at ....$20 each.

*Bronze turkeys are promoted on another page in George B.
Bayley's extensive Oakland Poultry Yards catalog. (Photo
courtesy California Historical Society Library)*

prices, and descriptions of a variety of equipment appurtenant to raising poultry. Galvanized wire netting in various-sized meshes is shown keeping chickens contained. Meat and vegetable choppers are touted as "invaluable where many fowls are kept." The listing of bone and shell mills ends with a poem called, "Owed to a Mill."

> The "WILSON MILL" we like full well,
> With bones it plays the Dickens.
> Our chickens eat the broken bones,
> And then we eat the chickens.
>
> No soft shelled eggs are ever laid
> By Biddy on our table,
> For every day she tries to lay
> As HARD as she is able.

Nothing a new or established poulterer might need appears to have been missing from Bayley's stock. It included food, thermometers, pills, carbolic nest eggs, caponizing instruments, vermin exterminators, feed troughs, water fountains, farm gates, and even poultry books and magazines. Bayley concluded his presentation of what the Oakland Poultry Yard would provide with a flyer for a new edition of his and C. J. Ward's book on western poultry care: "*The Pacific Coast Poulterer's Hand Book and Guide* for treating diseases of poultry, giving cause, symptoms and remedies for their care. Also, how to caponize fowls, and feed and rear chickens hatched in an incubator . . . Price, 40 cents, by mail, prepaid."

In addition to his extensive, all-inclusive approach to raising fancy poultry and his never ceasing passion for mountain climbing, he looked at every innovation toward better living that came his way. He was among the first to link his business with others by telephone.[17] The Oakland number for the poultry yard was *one four*, which indicates how early he saw a future for the telephone. There was already a line across the bay to San Francisco; he could keep in instant communication with his associates in the city.

Enthusiastic at being a part of the developing bay area culture, he expanded his collection of contemporary western art. He followed the exhibit of his artist friends' works to the 1893 Columbian Exposition in Chicago.[18] On his return he reported that it was a colossal exhibition and that everyone who went could see something that he would especially like. "My fad is art," he said, "and I spent most of my time in the art galleries."

At home Bayley integrated his ebullience with the gracious formality of Gertrude's household. In this paradoxical ménage close relatives and close friends were always welcome to find shelter and hospitality. A young friend from the East Coast stayed with the Bayleys until he established himself in business, married, moved out, and set up his own household for his growing family.[19]

The friend's daughter remembered calling on the Bayleys at her father's former home.[20] George would greet the little girl by picking her up, lifting her above his head, and calling out, "Thar she blows!", making her feel as if she truly were the spout of a whale. Then there would be much reminiscing between her father and George about the years they had spent on the Boston waterfront. A niece of George's also remembered calling at the Bayleys', when George asked her how her schoolwork progressed. He showed great interest in her repeated discouraged replies and tried to help her see the need for greater diligence.[21]

When his poultry business had a momentum of its own, he was tugged back to the daily commute to the city and its churning excitement. He took a post with a San Francisco drug and extract manufacturer, Merten, Moffitt, and Company.[22] Again, Charles Story, his brother-in-law, who was one of the officers of the firm, sponsored George.[23] Three years later George became president.[24]

A story handed down through his descendants indicates that no matter how sedentary his business activities may have been, he was always in condition for any climbing challenges.[25] One spring day on his morning trip across the bay he left his regular seat on the upper level of the ferryboat to get a cup of coffee. He had put down the flowers from his garden that he was taking to the office. When he returned to his place from the coffee counter, the flowers had disappeared. As was his custom, he prepared to disembark from the upper level. From where he stood he could see over the railing to the lower deck, which jutted further toward the bow than did the upper deck. A crowd had gathered to disembark to the ground level of the dock. The deck hands were securing the boat in the slip and starting to lower both gangplanks, the one above and the one below. Suddenly he spotted his bouquet in the clutch of a passenger standing almost directly beneath him. George jumped over the upper railing and landed ten feet down on the man carrying the flowers. With his mountaineering agility he rescued the flowers and carried them off to the office for which they had been intended.

His mountain-climbing drive was ever present and never satisfied. Every summer he and Gertrude visited Yosemite, and he had achieved one peak at the top of Rainier. But thoughts of the still-unvanquished north peak kept haunting him.

In 1885 a sea voyage that brought him in sight of the mighty mountain stirred him again.[26] He and Mrs. Bayley sailed to Alaska through the Inland Passage on the steamer *Ancon*. No Bayley excursion ever proved ordinary, and on the way home from this trip the ship's steam boiler blew up. The crew was able to maneuver the disabled craft to shore and anchor it in a cove. In the middle of the night eight sailors set out in a rowboat to row their skipper to the nearest help available. Two hundred and thirty miles away they reached Nanaimo on Vancouver Island.

While the ship was stalled for ten days, the shipwrecked passengers stayed on board. Most of them, including the Bayleys, were pioneers from the San Francisco Bay area and were used to the unexpected.[27] Some amused themselves on the ship, and during the daytime some went ashore in small boats to a close-by cove on Calvert Island, where they passed the time.[28] The island was populated only by Indians. Besides standing around watching the natives, the passengers had picnics, explorations, clambakes, mock courts, broom drills, and music, and they danced the Virginia reel on the beach. Those who stayed on the ship played cards and even published a newspaper, the *Ancon Crazy Quilt.*

At last, after days of waiting and not knowing, one of the marooned crew sighted a Nanaimo tugboat. The passengers sang, cried, and waved sheets and shawls to express their relief. The tug pulled the *Ancon* to its destination, where the passengers boarded another vessel. They sailed south through Puget Sound past Seattle and the Washington coast. Whether or not he could see the red flag he had hoisted two years before, a glance to the East would have revealed Rainier again and re-ignited George's desire to achieve the north peak of the "king of all the mountains."

NOTES

1. John Muir, "Summering in the Sierra," *Daily Evening Bulletin* (San Francisco, California) , August 26, 1876.

2. "Laid to Rest," *Morning Call* (San Francisco, California) , Vol. LXXV, No. 134, May 8, 1894, p. 3,

3. *Oakland Directory, 1888-1889.*

4. George Bayley, "More about Incubators," *Pacific Rural Press* (San Francisco) , May 20, 1882, p. 390.

5. "Artificial Production and Care of Fowls," *Pacific Rural Press* (San Francisco) , April 15, 1882.

6. I. L. Dias, "Notes on Iucubators," *Pacific Rural Press* (San Francisco) , April 29, 1882.

7. Bayley, "More about Incubators."

8. "California Poultry Association," *Pacific Rural Press* (San Francisco) , November 10, 1883, p. 405.

9. "The Poultry Show," *Pacific Rural Press* (San Francisco) , December 29, 1883, p. 566.

10. "California Poultry Association," *Pacific Rural Press* (San Francisco) , January 12, 1884.

11. *Oakland Directory, 1887-1888.*

12. "California Poultry Association," *Pacific Rural Press* (San Francisco) , April 18, 1885, p. 376.

13. "Annual Meeting of the California Poultry Association," *California Cackler* (San Francisco) , Vol. I, No. 9, April, 1886, p. 2.

14. "Incubators," *Pacific Rural Press* (San Francisco) , January 2, 1886, advertisement.

15. *Report of the Twentieth Industrial Exhibition of the Mechanics Institute of the City of San Francisco,* San Francisco, 1886, p. 98.

16. George Bayley, *Oakland Poultry Yards Price List of Fowls and Eggs*

and *Descriptive Circular of Breeding Stock* (Oakland, California: 1885) .

17. Bayley, *Oakland Poultry Yards.*

18. Unidentified newspaper clipping (from scrapbook kept by Bayley's daughter, Gertrude Bayley King) .

19. "Alameda County," *United States Census of 1880.*

20. Interview with Irene Bangs Barton.

21. Interview with Ethel Robertson Whiting.

22. *San Francisco Directory 1887.*

23. *San Francisco Directory 1886.*

24. *San Francisco Directory 1890.*

25. Interview with a grandson, Lionel Bayley King.

26. "The Ancon's Accident," *The Oregonian* (Portland, Ore.) , September 9, 1885, p. 3.

27. "Steamer Ancon," unidentified newspaper clipping (from scrapbook kept by Gertrude Bayley King) , 1885.

28. "Ten Days in Safety Cove, B.C.," unidentified newspaper clipping from scrapbook) , 1885.

CHAPTER TEN

King of All the Mountains

BEFORE BAYLEY MADE his final try for the north peak of Rainier in 1892, his appetite for the assault was whetted by Van Trump. In 1888 Bayley's friend John Muir set out from the bay area to Seattle armed with an introduction from Bayley to Van Trump.[1] Even though Muir had recently affronted Mrs. Bayley's dignity and hospitality, Bayley sponsored Muir.[2] Not too long before that Muir had accepted an invitation from Mrs. Bayley to dinner. Knowing full well that a dinner jacket was *de rigeur* at the Bayleys', Muir arrived in a red flannel shirt. The dinner party went off as planned, and the letter was written to Van Trump. Bayley bore no grudges.

Muir wanted to explore the glaciers on Mount Rainier. He planned to take along a photographer and an artist to get some pictures of the wonders of the mountain monarch. Using Bayley's recommendation, Muir prevailed on Van Trump to guide his group up the mountain.

After achieving the top and returning to Yelm, Van Trump wrote promptly to Bayley, providing a detailed account of the ascent and filling his report with enticements for Bayley to give the north peak another try:

> When the Ingraham-Muir-Keith party were here they found me (by reason of your direction), and though my business and my wife being without help made it really a dereliction of duty for me to leave home, they soon talked me

into the "mountain fever," and I went with them as guide to
the summit. . . .

I struck into our old line of ascent near Camp Ewing, and
from that on to the summit followed our old course. The
character of the snow was just the reverse of that we had. You
remember we had to cut steps occasionally on the steep snow
slopes between Camp Ewing and the great cliff, and also part
of the way in the snow wall to the left of the "gutter" by
which you and I scaled the brow of the mountain. That season there was fine, hummocky snow from Camp Ewing to the
brow of the mountain. This season there are no hummocks,
nor parallel upright sheets of ice, and no pinnacles of ice, as
when you and I climbed the slope of the summit, but clear,
hard, dazzling white snow, just rough enough to enable one
to get a good footing with caulks. The climbing from the top
of the "gutter" to the summit was splendid, and was accomplished in much less time than you and I did it in. This
season, however, there was more danger on the side of the
Summit, for if a climber had fallen and commenced to roll,
there would have been no stopping till one of the crevasses
had swallowed him, or till he plunged over the brow of the
mountain.[3]

Van Trump's letter recalled his and Bayley's previous experience:

There is much more snow in the craters, too, than when
you and Longmire and I spent that never-to-be-forgotten
night in one of them. The place where we slept (?) is completely snowed over, and could not have been found had it
not been for the hole which the steam has melted in the
canopy of ice and snow. Going as near as I could to the steaming hole and looking down, I saw a portion of the stone barrier we then built as a sort of a breakwind. We were scarcely
two hours on the summit.

And again Van Trump shared with Bayley his unrealized
longing for that mysterious north peak:

I wanted to visit the north peak, but no one would go with me. I never saw a crowd so anxious to get down to lower terra firma.

I was very desirous of doing the north peak, or Ta-ho-ma as Stevens and I named it, inasmuch as I had three times climbed the mountain, and for some moments I debated with myself (or with the spirit of precaution, reinforced by thoughts of the wife and the little ones) the question of remaining and going it alone to the north peak, or returning with my companions. Deferring at length to Muir's superior knowledge and experience, I gave up the long-cherished idea of visiting the virgin soil (or vestal snow) of the north peak. I gave a "longing, lingering look" at it as I joined Mr. Muir in his descent into the large crater to begin our journey down the mountain.

Despite Van Trump's enticing words, it was to be four more years before he and Bayley made their successful attempt to conquer the north peak. In 1892, determined to make a final and supreme effort to master the coveted peak, Van Trump kept his promise to Bayley. Van Trump wrote to invite his friend to join him that summer.

Van Trump was seeking the company of one of California's first conservation activists. In June of 1892, John Muir, hoping that he would "be able to do something for wildness, and make the mountains glad,"[4] enlisted among twenty-seven others his friend the "short man, or even shorter" to sign the articles of incorporation that established the Sierra Club.[5] They stated as their chief purpose: "To explore, enjoy and render accessible the mountain regions of the Pacific Coast; to publish authentic information concerning them; to enlist the support and cooperation of people and the government in preserving the forests and other natural features of the Sierra Nevada Mountains."[6] Politically the club was founded as a guardian for the Yosemite reserve, and it was natural that George Bayley would be a charter member. But this new expression of his dedication to the California mountains did not deter Bayley from his determination to conquer Rainier's north peak.

John Muir's party atop the summit of Mount Rainier, 1888. Left to right, Daniel Waldo Bass, Philemon Beecher Van Trump, John Muir (seated), N. O. Booth, and Edward Sturgis Ingraham. (Photo by Arthur Churchill Warner courtesy Photography Collection, University of Washington Library)

Conveniently, later that summer, Bayley was called to Portland, Oregon on business. He took his grown daughter, Gertrude, with him as far as the Van Trumps' house at Yelm, where she was to wait with Mrs. Van Trump until the climbers returned from their attempt at Rainier.

The two mountaineers set out from Yelm on August 16, each astride a pony and one leading a weighed-down packhorse. In three days they arrived at the highest meadow, the one nearest the line of perpetual snow, and set up their permanent camp. They tethered one pony, freed the other, and set out the next morning on foot, still leading the loaded packhorse, Oneonta. They planned to take him as far as was practicable. His load consisted of what the climbers could take on their backs. Each would have in addition to meager food rations a double blanket, an extra woolen undershirt and overshirt, an extra pair of woolen socks, and the regulation alpenstock. One would carry a hatchet, the other a seventy-five-foot rope.

The challenges of the approach and of the mountain itself were the same as they had been in 1883. The conditions of the snow and ice and weather differed a good deal. Van Trump left a detailed account of the entire expedition which was published in the *Sierra Club Bulletin* of May 1894. He compared the conditions on this trip with those they experienced on the previous ascent:

> Mountaineers and puffing steed now climbed for something more than a good mile over alternate fields of snow and patches of rock to a point where the spur we were ascending connected by a narrow tongue of loose shelving rock with one of the rocky ridges which extend up the mountain toward the south peak. When we reached this narrow tongue of loose rock, to get on which there was quite a jump-off from the spur we had ascended, we discussed whether we should take the horse any further. My companion was in favor of doing so, and it could easily have been done with a sure-footed cayuse used to climbing over rocks; but as the horse was heavy, and not a graduate in mountain climbing, I thought it best to dispense with him there. . . . We soon stripped One-

Longmire Springs, August 12, 1888. Henry Loomis is shown near the bath house, Mrs. James Longmire, second to the right. (Photo by Arthur Churchill Warner courtesy Photography Collection, University of Washington Library)

onta of his pack and halter, leaving him at perfect liberty to return or follow.... For about a half-mile from the point where the horse left us we climbed the ridge of rock extending up toward the south peak, then descended it on the left and got on to one of the three glaciers....

Where we crossed the glacier it was cut up with many crevasses, some of them wide and deep, and in threading our way among them, and in looking for "bridges" of ice on which to cross the larger and more dangerous ones, considerable time was occupied. When we finally reached the ledge of rock, 11,000 feet altitude, where we intended to spend the night, it was evening, and we were tired enough to stop. Selecting the spot that seemed the nearest level and the *softest* on this rocky point, we unrolled our blankets and prepared our mountain bed while it was yet light.... Our camping-site was on the edge of the Tahoma glacier, the main glacier of the west side of the mountain....[7]

With their spirit lamp and drinking cup they melted some ice to quench their thirst. Then they retired to prepare for the last push to the top:

Early in the morning following the cold and disagreeable night we spent in our stony bed at 11,000 feet, we got on the glacier and commenced climbing in a diagonal line upward toward the smooth central snowline already described. For more than four hours we toiled upward, threading our way among innumerable crevasses, now climbing along the sharp, icy edge of a wide one, where a single misstep would have hurled us down into its blue and yawning depths on the one hand, or on the other down its steep, icy side, to be swallowed by the next yawning crevasse below; again crossing other deep and wider-mouthed ones by means of natural ice-bridges spanning them; at other times leaping narrow ones, and occasionally crossing one and attaining its higher upper wall by means of a ladder which my companion, with sailor skill, constructed of our rope and alpenstocks.

When, as stated, we had toiled upward in this way for over

four hours, we had the inexpressible chagrin of finding ourselves in a wilderness of crevasses, so wide that there was no
practical way of crossing them. There was nothing to do but
retrace our steps and begin a new line of ascent in the desired
direction. This we did, and after a long and tedious effort,
during which we threaded a labyrinth of crevasses, we reached
the long-sought and smooth medial line of the glacier; but
there was no possible chance of reaching the summit before
nightfall. . . .

They were approaching the part of the mountain that would
cause this to be their last climb up Rainier:

It was early evening when we reached the foot of the steepest stretch of the ascent (a portion of it that my companion
will long remember) , namely, where the glacier flows from
over the rocky brow of the mountain, 1000 feet below its
actual summit. I supposed, from previous experience, that
we would have much tedious step-cutting at this point; but
much to our satisfaction we found the snow in such favorable
condition that our shoe-calks took good hold of the hard
snow, and, with the additional help of our alpenstocks, we
climbed without having to resort to much step-cutting. . . .

After traveling for some distance over a comparatively
gradual slope, with the north peak on our left and the middle
or Crater Peak on our right, we came to the foot of the dome
of the latter, turned our course southward, and began climbing the steep slope of Crater Peak. The night air was now
piercingly cold, August though it was, and our shoes, which
became soaked with water as the snow had melted on them
during the heat of the afternoon, now froze as hard as
boards. . . .

The two climbers were facing the most difficult part of the
the climb in pitch darkness. Van Trump described their meeting the challenge:

Now began the steep ascent of the north slope of Crater

Peak's dome. Occasionally we would come to a broad patch of peculiarly hard, glassy ice, caused, I think, by swirls of steam from the crater depositing moisture which the keen night air converted into sheets of glassy ice. Our shoe-calks seemed to make no impression on it, and many were the sudden falls we got; it was difficult at times to prevent our bodies from rolling down toward the dangerous brow of the mountain. Once my companion, in a sudden slip, had the coil of rope loosened from his grasp, and it rapidly slid down to the foot of the dome, where we regained it on our descent.

At last, at about 11 o'clock at night, we reached the rim of the small crater, and our climbing for the night was done. . . .

They knew even in the dim starlight where to bed down near the steam jets. Again they prepared drinking water, this time by melting ice over the steam. Van Trump compared this night with the one they had spent there nine years before:

In 1883, when Bayley and I, and our companion, James Longmire, in the morning climbed out of the crater, where we had steamed all night till our clothes were reeking with moisture, the fierce, cold wind in five minutes froze our clothing stiff, and we became so numbed with cold that the wind repeatedly prostrated us among the sharp rocks of the crater's rim, and for some time it seemed that we must succumb. This time the air in the morning was still calm, and the sun rose gloriously to convert the summit of Tahoma and its companion peaks into domes of burnished gold. We now revisited familiar points, and searched in particular for the lead plate we had left in the crater in 1883. We could not find it, though I had seen it in August, 1891, just where we left it. . . . We learned on reaching the lower country that a mountain-climber, who had visited the crater a week or two before us, had taken the plate away as a trophy, and to exhibit it as an evidence that he had reached the top.

After re-examining the craters all we cared to, we re-shouldered our packs and started for the north peak between 7 and 8 o'clock in the morning. We found the snow in good condition both for descending the middle peak and for climbing North Peak. We accomplished in a little less than two hours this feat, which we had long been desirous of accomplishing. . . .

We climbed to the very apex of its snowy summit. We met with one great disappointment. The whole of the landscape below us was blotted from view by a dense pall of mist and smoke, except where rents in the pall gave us but glimpses of it. Through several of these rents we caught glimpses of Puget Sound. . . .

From "Liberty Cap," or the snowy apex of North Peak, we descended about 80 feet to the bare rock below it on the west. Here to a projection of the rock we wired the tin-plate reflector, facing it toward Yelm. . . . Mr. Bayley deposited on this rock another lead plate with our names and the date and year engraved on it.

They had conquered the north peak, made it to the peak that crowned the "king of all the mountains." With evidence of their accomplishment marked by the securing of the plates, they began the descent on the morning of August 22. But a great mishap that marred the descent overshadowed the north peak victory.

In an interview with a newspaper reporter after his return to Oakland Bayley recounted his experience.[8] A copy of a clipping of the newspaper article published in the *Oakland Enquirer* on Friday, September 23, in that same year was saved by George's half-brother Frank in Seattle. Bayley had corrected, edited, and sent the clipping to a brother-in-law in Ohio who forwarded it to Frank.[9] The headline of the article read, "Like a Flash," with the subhead, "An Oaklander's Awful Slide Down Mt. Rainier— George B. Bayley Falls Over Two Thousand Feet in About Ten Seconds." Bayley's first mark on the clipping was to cross out "Ten" and write in " (about 40 I think) ."

Before answering the reporter's questions about the accident on the descent, Bayley as usual recalled the magnificent daybreak he beheld when he arose on top of the mountain on August 22, and the reporter chronicled it:

To the south could be seen Mt. Hood, Jefferson and
Adams, to the north stood out Mt. Baker and to the east the
Tatoosh range, while to the west they looked out on Puget
Sound and Tacoma in the distance.

The Bayley-edited story continues to say that shortly after
nine o'clock, alpenstocks in their hands, they began their descent:

Up and down the mountain side was one sheet of ice, and
only by digging heels and alpenstock through the surface
could a footing be maintained. They had proceeded but a
few hundred feet when suddenly Bayley's foot slipped under
him, and before he could recover himself he had fallen. In
the fall the alpenstock dropped from his hand, and like a
flash he shot down the mountain, disappearing in an instant
from the horrified gaze of his companion, to be found an hour
later, over two thousand feet below, on a narrow ledge seventy
feet down in a crevasse which narrowed to a mere crack some
200 feet lower.

The reporter asked Mr. Bayley to describe his sensations during the awful slide:

"When I first fell I struck on my side in the center of the
couloir down which we had started. Instead of rolling, however, my body just slid over the surface for the first 1500 feet,
then a whirl brought me in a sitting posture, and with my
heels dug in the ice in front of me, throwing up showers of
splintered ice, I shot 500 feet further, was hurled across a crevasse over twenty feet in width, striking the opposite side with
a crash that knocked me senseless on a narrow ledge of the
crevasse seventy feet beneath.

"My unconsciousness must have been only momentary,
however, for I had realized my position when my flask, which
had dropped from my pocket during the slide came whirling
over the crevasse, disappearing down the slope; my colored
glasses followed them, falling onto the ledge at my side.

Kernahan House, Succotash Valley, where George B. Bayley in 1892 recuperated for seven days after his fall of more than 2,000 feet into a crevasse while descending Mount Rainier. Left to right in 1888, young Kernahan, Joe Stampler, William Keith, John Muir, Mr. and Mrs. J. B. Kernahan, Henry Loomis, and the Kernahans' daughter. (Photo by Arthur Churchill Warner courtesy Photography Collection, University of Washington Library)

"When I had regained my senses, I moved my arms and legs
and was overjoyed to find them uninjured, but the moment
I attempted to rise a sharp pain in my side brought me to a
realization that some of my ribs were broken.

"Using extreme caution and making my way very slowly
and painfully, I managed to pass along the ledge to a wider
bench, where I awaited the coming of Van Trump.

The interview with George Bayley covered also his under-
statement describing the two friends' near-failure to return:

"Being provided with a rope, with his aid I succeeded in
clambering up the face of the crevasse.

"Ordinarily we would have made camp that afternoon, but
owing to my wounded condition, and the fact that Van
Trump went snow blind, progress was so slow, that we had
to spend the three succeeding nights on the bleak mountain
side, the two last nights in a drenching storm.

"When we finally reached camp, we found that two of our
three horses had wandered off in the storm, and with a single
animal we made the trip to Kernahan's, a clearing in the
forest seventeen miles from camp. From Mr. and Mrs. Kernahan I received the most careful attention, and after remaining
there seven days, I started for Yelm (fifty miles distant) on
horseback.

"At Yelm I took the train for Portland, and there received
medical attention."

Next to the article George wrote his general observation concerning the reporter's inaccuracies: "In the main correct, but
the reporter has not been able to confine himself to the literal
truth, which one would think sufficiently thrilling —."

Van Trump gave a less perfunctory, more emotional description, one fraught with the impact of the rescue on the rescuer.
His story of what happened on the morning of the twenty-
second and the days following said:

We began the descent of the mountain by the route we had

climbed it. When we were at the steepest part of the descent,
and where the surface of the snow was hard and icy, at a point
probably 2000 feet below the summit, my companion, who
was in the lead, stepped on an icy and treacherous place
where his shoe-calks seemed to be useless. His feet flew from
under him, and he fell with such suddenness and unexpected-
ness that he lost the grasp of his alpenstock and left it sticking
in the crest of snow where he had planted it when making
the faulty step. As soon as he struck the snow his body began
rolling, and he rolled with great velocity for some distance
down the steep, icy slope. Then by some means, probably by
his own efforts to that end, he managed to assume a sitting
posture, with his feet pointing down the mountain. He now
bravely endeavored to check his speed by striking his calked
shoe-heels into the icy snow-crust and using his gloved hands
as drags or brakes; but it was all in vain. His efforts may have
had the effect of preventing an acceleration of speed, but it
did not stay his fearful progress down the mountain-side.

It will be remembered that it was stated earlier in these
pages that there was a smooth medial pathway up the glacier
from a certain point, toward which smooth line we ascended
in an oblique direction from the labyrinth of crevasses at the
side of the glacier. Now, it was directly down over this smooth
pathway that my companion was involuntarily descending
with such fearful rapidity, and toward a point where its
smoothness was terminated by crevasses which crossed it.
About 600 or 700 yards below the place where he lost his footing the first of these crevasses stretched across the smooth
snow-line. I remembered noting, as we passed around the far
end of it in ascending, how broad and deep it was. I saw that
it was inevitable that he would be lost in this crevasse unless
he could succeed in stopping his progress before he reached its
yawning mouth. From where I stood there seemed to be quite
a broad strip of snow in front of the crevasse that was comparatively level. My one hope was—and no doubt such was the
thought and hope that filled his mind—that the snow on this
level stretch in front of the crevasse would be so softened by
the sun's heat as to make successful his efforts to stop his

progress; but, as I gazed, I saw his body pass over the first of this level space, with lessened speed it is true, but with velocity enough to carry him to the crevasse. Nearer and nearer to that yawning crevasse did his body approach, till at last I saw it go over the brink and pass out of sight.

Never shall I forget my feeling of horror as I stood, spellbound, watching my friend's body approaching that fearful crevasse. I felt morally certain that when he disappeared from view his body lay a mangled corpse at the bottom of it. At first horror at his fate crowded all thought of self out of my mind; but with the re-action that followed came the thought, or self-asked question, "Can you pass with safety the fatal spot where your friend fell, or will you, too, fall and speed helplessly to and into that insatiable crevasse?" Taking my friend's alpenstock, from an inexplicable feeling that I ought to do so—for it certainly was going to incommode me rather than be of any benefit—I began to descend slowly and cautiously. . . . At last I reached the crevasse, but some distance to the left of the point where my friend had disappeared over its edge. This was owing to the oblique line of my descent to avoid the danger of a fall which would have been more likely to happen in a direct descent of the steep, icy slope. Approaching the edge of the crevasse, I called my friend loudly by name, but with no hope of getting any reply.

To my great surprise, and no less joy, I got a feeble answer from him, and almost underneath where I stood.

Passing around the end of the crevasse, still considerably to the left, I got over to the side on which the ledge was and directly over the place where he was standing. Letting one end of the rope down to him, I managed to help him out and over some huge blocks of ice that lay between the end of the crevasse and the line of descent to our 11,000-foot camp. My companion when he fell was carrying his coat slung over one shoulder, and I think when his body struck the ledge of ice upon which he lodged, this coat broke the force of the blow, and probably was the means of saving his life. When he emerged from the crevasse, my companion was as pale as a sheet and suffering great pain, but with great pluck and en-

A climbing party crosses the Nisqually River in 1895. (Photo by Arthur Churchill Warner courtesy Photography Collection, University of Washington Library)

durance, made the long and toilsome tramp to camp. We used
the rope in descending the remaining dangerous slopes.

Owing to Bayley's condition necessitating cautious traveling, to the large number of crevasses to be crossed, to the still
larger number to be wound around or circumvented, and to
the additional fact that I was carrying both packs now, our
progress toward the 11,000-foot camp was slow and tedious,
and it was nearly sundown when we reached it. The next
morning (23rd) the steep snowfield down which we had to
journey was hard and slippery and my companion did not
dare to travel over it till the sun had softened the surface of
the snow—for a fall now would be very disastrous to him. The
sun did not soften the snow till nearly noon.

We now started again, after throwing out of the packs
everything not absolutely needed. So slowly did we have to
travel that not till nearly sundown did we step off the glacier
which we first crossed in beginning the ascent. Just before we
left the glacier clouds began to roll up from the south, and
when we reached *terra firma* again we were in a thick, driving
mist, or, rather, we were enveloped in the clouds. Soon every
rock, bush and tree a dozen feet away vanished from sight as
completely as though they never had existed, and the wind
began blowing hard from the south.

It now became apparent to us that we could not find our
way to permanent camp in that obscuring mist before night
set in, so we decided to camp again on the mountain side.
Finding as suitable a place for our camp as I could, I laid in
a supply of wood, and after our frugal meal improvised a tent
with our alpenstocks, rope and one of our double blankets.
The wind kept increasing during the night, and shook our
tent fearfully, and often I got up and out to put an additional
bowlder on the end of the blanket, to keep it from blowing
away, it did not rain or snow, as we feared it would, but in
the morning the obscuring mist of clouds remained. We
waited till late in the forenoon for it to clear off, and then,
despairing of it, we started for our permanent camp. In descending the spur of the mountain, up which we took the
pack-horse on the 20th, we several times lost our course in the

blinding fog, and when we finally reached our long-sought
tent it was late in the afternoon. The first thing done was to
make my companion a comfortable bed; the next was to look
after the horses, and finally to get supper—for we were hungry
as wolves.

And now I found our picketed pony in a sad plight. She
had evidently, soon after we left on the 20th, caught her lariat
in a small bush which had escaped our notice as being within
reach of her tether, and had gone round and round it till her
nose almost touched the bush, and there she had been held a
prisoner, without food or water, and had been the helpless
prey of myriads of flies and mosqitoes during the heat of the
day for two days or more. Nearly the whole of her body was
covered with sores or crusted with blood, where numerous
horseflies had been feasting on her. I had to give her water in
small quantities, to prevent her killing herself with over-
drinking in her water-famished condition. Then a prospecting tour of the neighboring parks developed the comforting
fact that we were in all probability minus one pony and the
packhorse—for they were nowhere to be seen.

That night my eyes began to pain me, and the next morning when the sun was shining (for the clouds had cleared
away without giving the threatened storm) , it was with difficulty that I could use them, and I became aware of the fact
that I was having a touch at least of "snow-blind." As soon as
I could, on the morning of the 25th, I started out on a final
search for the lost animals. Nowhere in the mountain meadows could I find the missing pony, but I came upon Oneonta
more than a mile from camp. As I approached him, with a
small pan of tempting oats in my hand, he watched me with
a strange and suspicious eye, and when-ever I tried to get near
enough to lay my hand on him he bounded away with a snort.
Round and round I followed him, calling, coaxing and whee-
dling, but all in vain.

I went back to camp in no amiable frame of mind—for I
very well knew that this whim of Oneonta and the disappear-
ance of the other pony would necessitate the abandonment of
our tent and provisions for the present, and a journey on foot,

A climbing party descending from the summit of Mount Rainier in 1895. (Photo by Arthur Churchill Warner courtesy Photography Collection, University of Washington Library)

for me, to the settlement. When I got back to camp I informed my companion of the state of affairs, and we at once prepared to start for my friend J. B. Kernahan's, in the Succotash Valley, 15 miles distant. The pony (Nellie) was saddled, my companion was helped to mount her, and we moved off slowly—for the pony was anything but strong after her long fast, and my companion, in his condition, would not stand much jolting.

We arrived at Palisade Farm [Kernahan's] late at night. The last 3 miles of the journey were traveled in such utter darkness that my companion could not see the road nor even the head of the pony he was riding, yet she carried him safely over the mountain road and never stumbled once.

We received a hospitable welcome at Palisade Farm. My companion's broken ribs were set and skillfully bandaged, and the disabled mountaineer was kindly and carefully nursed back to health. During the several days that I spent at Palisade Farm to recruit (sic) , our missing horses, tent and provisions were brought in by a party which we sent out for them. After 8 days' sojourn at Palisade Farm, Mr. Bayley returned to Yelm, our starting-point, where I had preceded. Thus ended our final, but almost tragical, ascent of the North Peak of Tahoma.[10]

For two years Bayley worked to "make the mountains glad." His near-defeat by the powerful Rainier did not lessen his admiration for its natural wonder nor his eagerness to conserve its challenge and beauty for others. Along with his climbing friends Muir and Van Trump, Bayley was among five men selected to represent the Sierra Club in meeting with other conservation committees to prepare a memorial to Congress recommending a national park to include Mount Rainier.[11]

Bayley's life ended before the memorial reached the Congress and before the *Sierra Club Bulletin* told the details of his last climb to the top of Rainier. While the final proof of Mr. Van Trump's narrative was being read at the foot of Mount Tamalpais on the afternoon of April 30, 1894, George Bayley made an ascent in the elevator at his place of business in San Francisco, was caught between the elevator and the floor above, and was killed instantly.[12]

No one witnessed the accident.[13] No one knew how it happened. Toward the end of the workday afternoon some of his employees at the Merten Manufacturing Company at 210 Davis Street in San Francisco missed their employer from the front office. They supposed that he had gone home. When two of them went to the rear of the three-story building to hoist some goods up the open freight elevator to the second floor, they discovered his body between the floor of the elevator and the ceiling above it. His head was jammed between the two. His skull was fractured; the big veins of the neck burst. George Bayley was no more.

Although a coroner's jury found a verdict of accidental death, the coroner refused to accept the decision. Because there was no direct evidence of an accident, the official ruled that the jurors should have found that death was from unknown causes.[14] In spite of Bayley's reputation for having a passion for living, witnesses were asked if they had ever heard Mr. Bayley speak of suicide. They all replied that he was of cheerful disposition and that they knew of no business complications. After some further court proceedings the State Supreme Court ordered the insurance companies to pay Mrs. Bayley in full for the policies that her husband had carried.[15] The total of $165,000 was the largest settlement paid so far in the 44-year history of the State of California.

A part of George Bayley's legacy to his wife and son and daughter was the poignant irony of their having to accept that a man who so many times had risked his life against the whims of nature had fallen the victim of pure, mechanical accident. The threats, the caprices, the antagonisms, and the resistances of nature took no part in the final accident. Death came at the hand of a contraption of man in surroundings well sheltered by the appurtenances of civilization.

George Bayley's death would stand as a symbol of the irony in destiny, his life as a tribute to man's response to the inviting environment beyond his immediate orbit. Repeatedly nature and progress invited him. The sea invited an inquiring boy. The expanding West invited an adventurer; San Francisco's business world a thrifty Yankee. Oakland invited a homesteader; the market for fancy poultry a husbandman; San Francisco's art movement a connoisseur; the literary magazines a writer. The mountains invited a naturalist; Yosemite an explorer; Mount Rainier a true mountaineer. George Bayley had accepted; he had participated; and he had contributed.

The "spice of danger" could lure him no more, and only posterity would experience "the delicious after-taste" of his adventures and contributions.

NOTES

1. "Letter from P. B. Van Trump to George B. Bayley, dated August 26, 1888," *Tribune* (Oakland, California) , Vol. CXXXI, Nos. 23, 30, 37, and 44, July 23, 1939.

2. Interview with Ethel Robertson Whiting.

3. "Letter from P. B. Van Trump, August 26, 1888."

4. Holway Jones, *John Muir and the Sierra Club: The Battle for Yosemite* (San Francisco: Sierra Club, 1965) , p. 9.

5. Jones, *John Muir and the Sierra Club*, p. 174.

6. Jones, *John Muir and the Sierra Club*, p. 173.

7. P. B. Van Trump, "Mount Tahoma," *Sierra Club Bulletin* (San Francisco), Vol. I, No. 4 (May 1894), pp. 109-32; hereafter cited as Van Trump, "Mount Tahoma."

8. "Like a Flash, an Oaklander's Awful Slide Down Mount Rainier," *Oakland Enquirer*, September 23, 1892. This account is used hereafter without citation.

9. Frank S. Bayley, letter to Mrs. H. Hyer Whiting (Seattle, Washington) , January 21, 1938.

10. Van Trump, "Mount Tahoma."

11. Aubrey L. Haines, *Mountain Fever, Historic Conquests of Rainier* (Portland, Ore.: Oregon Historical Society, 1962) , pp. 174–75.

12. "A Sad End, George Bayley's Fate Mourned by His Friends," *Oakland Tribune*, Vol. XXXVII, No. 96, May 1, 1894, p. 3.

13. "Two Fatal Accidents," *Evening Daily Bulletin* (San Francisco) , May 1, 1894, p. 2.

14. "The Bayley Will, The Entire Estate Is Left to the Widow," *Oakland Enquirer*, Vol. XXIV, No. 109, May 8, 1894.

15. "Widow Will Get the Insurance," unidentified newspaper clipping from scrapbook kept by Gertrude Bayley King.

Bibliography

Books and Pamphlets

Annals of the Bohemian Club, Vol. I. San Francisco, 1880.

Bacon, Edwin M., ed. *Boston Illustrated: A Familiar Guide to Boston and Its Neighborhood.* Boston, Mass.: Houghton Mifflin Co., 1893.

Baker, Eleanor Johnson. *A Genealogy of the Descendants of William Johnson of Charlestown, Massachusetts.* Newburyport Press, Inc., 1969.

Bayley, William H., and Oliver Jones. *History of the Marine Society of Newburyport, Massachusetts from Its Incorporation in 1722 to the Year 1906.* 1906.

Bosqui, Edward. *Memoirs of Edward Bosqui.* Oakland, Calif.: Holmes Book Co., 1952.

Boston Annual Advertiser 1846.

Boston City Directory, 1840–1844, 1847–1849, 1865.

California State Gazetteer and Business Directory, 1890.

Coffin, Joshua. *A Sketch of the History of Newbury, Newburyport, and West Newbury.* Boston, 1845.

Congregational Year-Book of 1917.

Constitution, By-Laws, List of Members, Catalogue of Library and Rules of the School of Design of the San Francisco Art Association. San Francisco, 1878, p. 38.

Currier, John J. *History of Newburyport, Massachusetts.* Newburyport, Mass.: The Author, 1906.

————. *Ould Newberry: Historical and Biographical Sketches.* Boston: Damrell and Upham, 1896.

Elwell, Edward H. *Portland and Vicinity.* Portland, Me.: Loring, Short & Hermon, and W. S. Jones, 1876.

Emery, Sarah Anna. *Reminiscences of a Nonagenarian.* Newburyport, Mass.: William H. Huse & Co., 1879.

Farquhar, Francis P. *History of the Sierra Nevada.* Berkeley and Los Angeles, Calif.: University of California Press in Collaboration with the Sierra Club, 1965.

Genealogy and Local History: Goodspeed's Catalogue 520. Boston, Mass.: Goodspeed's Bookshop, Inc., no date.

General Catalogue of Bowdoin College and the Medical School of Maine: A Biographical Record of Alumni and Officers, 1794–1950. Brunswick, Me., 1950.

Gudde, Erwin G. *California Place Names: The Origin and Etymology of Current Geographical Names.* Berkeley and Los Angeles, Calif.: University of California Press, 1969.

Haines, Aubrey L. *Mountain Fever: Historic Conquests of Rainier.* Portland, Ore.: Oregon Historical Society, 1962.

Hittell, John S. *The Commerce and Industries of the Pacific Coast of North America.* San Francisco: A. L. Bancroft & Co., 1882.

Huel, John T., ed. *Centennial Celebration: An Account of the Municipal Celebration of the One Hundredth Anniversary of the Incorporation of the Town of Portland, July 4th, 5th, and 6th, 1886.* Portland, Me.: Owen, Strout & Co., 1886.

Hutchings, J. M. *Heart of the Sierras: The Yo Semite Valley, Both Historical and Descriptive: And Scenes by the Way.* Yo Semite Valley, Calif.: Old Cabin, 1886.

Insurance Maps. Oakland, Vol. 1. New York: Sanborn Map and Publishing Co., Ltd., 1889.

Jones, Holway R. *John Muir and the Sierra Club: The Battle for Yosemite.* San Francisco, Calif.: Sierra Club, 1965.

Kehrlein, Oliver. *The Sierra Nevada: The Range of Light,* ed. Roderick Peattie. New York: Vanguard Press, 1947.

Lloyd, B. E. *Lights and Shades in San Francisco.* San Francisco, Calif.: printed by A. L. Bancroft & Co., 1876.

Lyman, George D. *Ralston's Ring: California Plunders the Comstock Lode.* New York: Charles Scribner's Sons, 1945.

Marquand, John P. *Timothy Dexter Revisited.* Boston: Little, Brown and Company, 1960.

Merrill, Rev. Samuel H. *Discourse Occasioned by the Death of Capt. Christopher T. Bayley, Preached in Portland,* May 17,

1857. Randolph, Mass., 1857.

Molenaar, Dee. *The Challenge of Rainier: A Record of the Explorations and Ascents, Triumphs and Tragedies, on the Northwest's Greatest Mountain.* Seattle, Wash.: The Mountaineers, 1971.

Muir, John. *John of the Mountains: The Unpublished Journals of John Muir,* ed. Linnie Marsh Wolfe. Boston, Mass.: Houghton Mifflin, 1938.

_____. *South of Yosemite: Selected Writings by John Muir,* ed. Frederic R. Gunsky. Garden City, N.Y.: Natural History Press, 1968.

_____. *The Yosemite.* Garden City, N.Y.: Natural History Library, Doubleday & Company, 1962.

New England Historical and Genealogical Register, Index of Persons. New England Historic Genealogical Society, 1907. Vols. 1–50.

New York City Directory 1848–1850, 1855–1856, 1859, 1860–1862, 1866–1875.

Newburyport Economic Development Commission. *A Walking Tour of Newburyport.*

Newell, Gordon, and Joe Williamson. *Pacific Coastal Liners.* Seattle, Wash.: Superior Publishing Co., 1959.

Oakland and Alameda Directory 1875–76.

Oakland Directory 1875–82, 1884–1889, 1891, 1893, 1894.

Pettingell, John Mason. *A Pettingell Genealogy.* Boston, Mass.: New England Historical Society, 1906.

Portland, Maine, City Directory 1856–57, 1888.

Price, J. *Buyers Manual.* 1872. (From California Historical Society.)

Rasmussen Louis J. *San Francisco Ships Passenger Lists.* Vol. I. Baltimore: Deford, 1965.

Report of the Tenth Industrial Exhibition under the Auspices of the Mechanics, of the City of San Francisco. San Francisco: Leo Eloesser, Steam Book, Card and Job Printer, 1876.

Report of the Twentieth Industrial Exhibition of the Mechanics Institute of the City of San Francisco. San Francisco: P. J. Thomas, Printer, 1886.

Roper, Steve. *A Climber's Guide to Yosemite Valley.* San Francisco, Calif.: Sierra Club, 1964.

Rossiter, William S., ed. *Days and Ways in Old Boston.* Boston, Mass.: Stearns, 1915.

Russell, Carl Parcher. *One Hundred Years in Yosemite: The Story of a Great Park and Its Friends.* Yosemite National Park, Calif.: Yosemite Natural History Association, 1959.

San Francisco Business Directory 1856.

San Francisco Directory 1854, 1856, 1862–1868, 1870–1894.

San Francisco Social Manual 1884.

Sargent, Shirley. *Pioneers in Petticoats: Yosemite's Early Women 1856—1900.* Los Angeles, Calif.: Trans-Anglo Books, 1966.

Sawyier, Nathaniel, and Joseph Burbeen Walker. *A Genealogy of Some of the Descendants of William Sawyer of Newbury, Massachusetts.* Manchester, N.H.: W. E. Moore, 1889.

Ship Registers of the District of Newburyport, Massachusetts, 1789–1870. Salem, Mass.: The Essex Institute, 1937.

Ship Registers of the District of Salem and Beverly, Massachusetts 1789–1900. Salem, Mass.: The Essex Institute, 1906.

Simpson's Boston Directory, 1837.

Smith, Mrs. E. Vale. *History of Newburyport: From the Earliest Settlement of the Country to the Present Time.* Newburyport, 1854.

Stockton [California] *Directory 1876.*

Vital Records of Newbury, Massachusetts to the End of the Year 1849, Vol. I, *Births;* Vol. II, *Marriages and Deaths.* Salem, Mass.: The Essex Institute, 1911.

Voge, Hervey H., ed. *A Climber's Guide to the High Sierra.* San Francisco, Calif.: Sierra Club, 1965.

Warren, Josephine. *The 'Yosemite' by M.I.W. 1866.* San Francisco, Calif.: Society of Pioneers, 1942.

Willis, William. *The History of Portland from 1632 to 1864.* 2nd ed. Portland, Me.: Bailey and Noyes, 1865.

Winsor, Justin, ed. *The Memorial History of Boston Including Suffolk County, Massachusetts 1630–1880.* Vol. IV. Boston, Mass.: James R. Osgood & Co., 1881.

Wolfe, Linnie Marsh. *Son of the Wilderness: The Life of John Muir.* New York: Alfred A. Knopf, 1945.

Wood, M. W. *History of Alameda County, California.* Oakland, Calif.: M. W. Wood, 1883.

Newspaper and Magazine Articles

Bayley, George B. "Eleven Days in the High Sierra." *Daily Independent* (Stockton, Calif.), December 21, 1878. Also in San

Francisco *Argonaut,* December 21, 1878.

_____. "More about Incubators." *Pacific Rural Press,* May 20, 1882.

_____. "Mount Tahoma." *Overland Monthly,* VIII (September 1886).

_____. "Mount Tahoma." *Every Sunday* (Tacoma, Wash.), undated.

Bohemian Records 1881–1907. "Society: Ladies' Jinks at the Bohemian Club." October 22, 1888.

California Cackler. Vol. 4, No. 5 (1888).

California Cackler. "Annual Meeting of the California Poultry Association." Vol. 1, No. 9 (April 1886), p. 2.

California Cackler. "Poultry Awards at the State Fair." Vol. 2, No. 3 (1886), p. 10.

California Cackler. "California Poultry Association—No Show This Year." Vol. 2, No. 4 (1886), p. 8.

California Cackler. "The Next Poultry Show in California." Vol. 3, No. 2 (1887).

Daily Alta California. February 1, 1889.

Daily Evening Bulletin (San Francisco). "Summering in the Sierra." September 6, 1876.

Daily Evening Bulletin (San Francisco). February 1, 1889.

Daily Evening Bulletin (San Francisco). "Across the Bay: Death of John D. Arthur, A Well-Known Pioneer." January 31, 1889.

Daily Independent (Stockton). "The High Sierra." December 21, 1878.

Daily Oregonian. "Mount Tacoma." October 1, 1883.

Dias, I. L. "Still More about Incubators." *Pacific Rural Press,* June 10, 1882.

Evening Daily Bulletin (San Francisco). "Two Fatal Accidents." May 1, 1894.

Evening Daily Bulletin (San Francisco). "Across the Bay." May 2, 1894.

Evening Daily Bulletin (San Francisco). "Large Life Insurance." May 3, 1894.

Evening Transcript (Boston). July 1, 1844.

Examiner (San Francisco). "Dead in the Elevator." May 1, 1894.

Farquhar, Francis P. "Naming America's Mountains: The Sierra Nevada of California." *American Alpine Journal.* New

York: American Alpine Club, 1964.

Fuller, Fay. "Mount Tahoma—Historical Sketch of All Successful Climbers—Names and Dates." *Every Sunday* (Tacoma,
Wash.) , August 23, 1890.

_____. "A Trip to the Summit." *Every Sunday* (Tacoma,
Wash.) , August 23, 1890.

Gazette (Mariposa, Calif.) . "Arrivals in Yosemite Valley." July
6, 1866.

Gazette (Mariposa, Calif.) . "Wanderings in Yo Semite Valley."
September 14, 1867.

Gazette (Mariposa, Calif.) . July 6, 1901.

James, George. "Mount Tahoma: Its Ascent in June, 1884, by
a Snohomish Party." *The Daily Ledger* (Tacoma, Wash.) ,
November 26, 1892.

Kautz, A. V. "Mount Tahoma, The First Attempt by White
Men to Reach its Highest Peaks." *Washington Republican*
(Steilacoom) , July 24, 1857. (Also published in *Every Sunday*
[Tacoma, Wash.], undated.)

Ledger (Tacoma, Wash.) . "Conquering the Giant." September
12, 1892.

Leonard, Richard M., and David R. Brower. "A Climber's
Guide to the High Sierra, Part IV, Yosemite Valley." *Sierra
Club Bulletin,* Vol. XXV (February 1940) , pp. 41 ff.

Morning Call (San Francisco) . "The Death of John D. Arthur
on Tuesday Evening." Vol. LXV, No. 62, January 31, 1889,
p. 7.

Morning Call (San Francisco) . "Died. Bayley, George R. [sic]."
May 2, 1894.

Morning Call (San Francisco) . "Laid to Rest: George Bayley's
Life Insured for $165,000." Vol. LXXV, No. 134, May 8, 1894,
p. 3.

Muir, John. "The Kings River Valley." *Daily Evening Bulletin*
(San Francisco) , August 13, 1875.

_____. "Summering in the Sierra—A New Yosemite—The
King's River Valley." *Daily Evening Bulletin* (San Francisco) , August 18, 1875.

_____. "Mount Whitney." *Daily Evening Bulletin* (San Fran-
cisco) , August 24, 1875.

_____. "Summering in the Sierra." *Daily Evening Bulletin*
(San Francisco) , September 15, 1875.

_____. "Summering in the Sierra: The Summit of South

Dome." *Daily Evening Bulletin* (San Francisco), September 6, 1876.

_____. "The Kings River Valley." *Sierra Club Bulletin,* XXVI (February 1941), pp. 1–8.

New York Evening Post. Saturday, May 25, 1844.

Oakland Enquirer. "The Bayley Will, The Entire Estate is Left to the Widow." Vol. XXIV, No. 109, May 8, 1894.

Oakland Enquirer. "Distressing. Death of George B. Bayley of This City. He Was Caught in His Own Elevator and His Life Crushed Out." May 1, 1894.

Oakland Enquirer. "Like a Flash, an Oaklander's Awful Slide Down Mount Rainier." September 23, 1892.

Oakland Tribune. May 8, 1894.

Oakland Tribune. "The Knave." July 23, 1939.

Oakland Tribune. "A Sad End, George Bayley's Fate Mourned by His Friends." Vol. XXXVII, No. 96, May 1, 1894.

Oakland Tribune. "Sad Services." May 2, 1894.

Pacific Historian. August 1962.

Pacific Rural Press. Advertisements, 1871–1886 *passim.*

Pacific Rural Press. "Poultry Notes: Choice Poultry Yards." March 25, 1871, p. 185.

Pacific Rural Press. "Choice Poultry." April 8, 1871.

Pacific Rural Press. "Poultry Notes: Improving our Poultry Stock." May 13, 1871.

Pacific Rural Press. "White Leghorn Fowls." January 13, 1872, p. 1.

Pacific Rural Press. "Poultry Notes: Practical Poultry Growing." March 1, 1873, p. 137.

Pacific Rural Press. "Thoroughbred Poultry." March 8, 1873.

Pacific Rural Press. "The Bronze Turkey." April 5, 1873, p. 217.

Pacific Rural Press. "Description of Light and Dark Brahmas." April 12, 1873.

Pacific Rural Press. "Practical Poultry Growing: Bronze Turkeys." April 26, 1873.

Pacific Rural Press. "The White Leghorn." May 10, 1873.

Pacific Rural Press. "Artificial Production and Care of Fowls." April 15, 1882.

Pacific Rural Press. "Poultry Yard: Notes on Incubators." April 29, 1882.

Pacific Rural Press. "California Poultry Association." November 10, 1883.

Pacific Rural Press. "A Poultry Exhibition." November 10, 1883.

Pacific Rural Press. "Poultry Notes." December 22, 1883.

Pacific Rural Press. "A Return to the Chicken Business." December 29, 1883.

Pacific Rural Press. "The Poultry Show." December 29, 1883.

Pacific Rural Press. "California Poultry Association." January 12, 1884.

Pacific Rural Press. "California Poultry Association." October 18, 1884.

Pacific Rural Press. "California Poultry Association's Second Annual Exhibition." January 31, 1885.

Pacific Rural Press. "The Poultry Premiums." February 14, 1885.

Pacific Rural Press. "California Poultry Association." April 18, 1885.

Pacific Rural Press. "Poultry Association Meeting." October 10, 1885.

Pacific Rural Press. "A Premium Bronze Turkey." January 2, 1886.

Pacific Rural Press. "The Poultry Show." January 16, 1886.

Pacific Rural Press. "The Poultry Show. An Official Award of Premiums." January 23, 1886.

Pioneer (San Jose, Calif.). January 24, 1898.

Portland, Maine, *Daily Eastern Argus.* "Died." May 12, 1857.

Portland (Maine) *Transcript.* "Deaths." May 16, 1857.

Portland *Oregonian.* "The Ancon's Accident." September 9, 1885.

San Francisco *Bulletin.* "Marriage." August 8, 1867.

San Francisco *Daily Alta California.* "Married." August 8, 1867.

San Francisco *Daily Examiner.* "Married." August 8, 1867.

Schuyler, James D. "Mountaineering about Yosemite: A Climb to the top of Yo Semite Falls." *Daily Independent* (Stockton, Calif.), July 11, 1877.

————. "The Ascent of Mount Starr King." *Daily Independent* (Stockton, Calif.), July 12, 1877.

Old Sequal (as related to J. Preston Moore). "Mount Tahoma, Its Ascent in June, 1884, by a Snohomish Party, The Legend of the Mountain." *Snohomish Eye,* September 6, 1884. (Also published in *Every Sunday* [Tacoma, Wash.], November 26, 1892.)

Times (Seattle). "What-A-Man Named Bayley! Move on to

Recognize Virtually Anonymous One." July 7, 1935.

Times (Seattle). "Enter, Mr. Bayley! Mystery Climber is Known." July 11, 1935.

Van Trump, P. B. "Above the Clouds, Mt. Rainier Revisited." Unidentified newspaper, Olympia, Washington Territory, September 8, 1883.

_____. "Mount Rainier Revisited!" *Transcript* [Olympia, Washington Territory], September 8, 1883.

Van Trump, P. B. "Conquering the Giant, Perilous Ascent and Descent of Mount Tacoma Thrillingly Described." *Ledger* (Tacoma, Wash.), September 12, 1892.

_____. "Names of the Great Mountain Discussed by Van Trump." *The Tacomian*, December 24, 1892.

_____. "Mount Tahoma. The North Peak—Van Trump's First Attempt to Reach It in August, 1891." *The Tacomian*, February 25, 1893.

_____. "Up the Mountain High." *The Daily Ledger* (Tacoma, Wash.), April 10, 1893.

_____. "Mount Tahoma." *Sierra Club Bulletin*, Vol. I (1894), pp. 109–132.

_____. "Death of George B. Bayley." *Ledger* (Tacoma, Wash.), May 17, 1894.

_____. [Letter to George B. Bayley, dated August 26, 1888.] *Tribune* (Oakland, Calif.), July 23, 30; August 6, 30, 1939.

_____. "The Sage of Yelm Speaks." *The Tacomian*, undated.

_____, and George B. Bayley. "Mount Tahoma, Exploration of the North Peak." *Every Sunday* (Tacoma, Wash.), March 11, 1893.

_____, James Longmire, and George B. Bayley. "Mount Takhoma." *Every Sunday* (Tacoma, Wash.), November 5, 1892.

_____. "Mount Takhoma." *Every Sunday* (Tacoma, Wash.), November 12, 1892.

Government Records

Arthur, Jacob C. *Certified Copy Last Will and Testament.* Columbia County Courthouse, Hudson, New York.

Bayley, George B. *Last Will and Testament.* June 2, 1882.

Bayley, G. K., Respondent, *v.* Employers' Liability Assurance Corporation, Appellant. S.F. No. 857. In Bank. July 12, 1899. [Supreme Court decision]

Biographical Directory of the American Congress 1774–1961. U.S. Government Printing Office, 1961.

Deed Book WW [County of Columbia, N.Y.], p. 244.

Monthly Weather Review, Mount Washington Observatory, N.H., Progress Report. Washington, D.C.: U.S. Department of Agriculture, Weather Bureau, January 1934.

Probate Proceedings in the Matter of the Estate of George Blake Bayley, Deceased. Superior Court of the County of Alameda, State of California, Dept. 1—Probate. May 21, 1894.

San Francisco County Census, July, 1852.

United States Census: Alameda County, California, 1880.

United States Census: Boston, Massachusetts, 1840.

United States Census: Somerville, Massachusetts, 1850.

Voter Registrations, San Francisco, 1866.

Unpublished and Private Papers

Bayley Family *Bible.*

Bayley, Christopher T. Passenger List of the Schooner *Mary.* March 11, 1830.

Bayley, Frank S., Sr. Letter to Mrs. H. Hyer Whiting (Seattle, Washington). January 21, 1938.

Bayley, George B. Inscription in Cosie Hutchings' *Autograph Book.* August 19, 1890.

Bayley, George B. Photograph Album.

Bohemian Club. "Members of the Bohemian Club, 2nd Series." Photograph by Bradley & Rulofson. San Francisco, Calif., 1873.

Bohemian Club. Photograph of Members. Undated.

Bowdoin College Library, Special Collections. Biographical information on Frank T. Bayley.

Caledonia Silver Mining Company Stock Certificate. At Wells Fargo Bank History Room, San Francisco, 1879.

Grand Register of the Cosmopolitan. Yosemite Museum, June 1866, August 12, 1867, July 1873, June 1874, June 1877, June 1881.

MacDonald, W. G. Research compiled for the American President Lines. (Sent by Albert Harmon of the San Francisco

Maritime Museum.)

Morareidge, Annabel B. Personal correspondence. December 22, 1971.

Mountain View Cemetery. Records. Oakland, California.

Mountain View House Hotel Register. At Miss Peregoy's, Lodi, California, 1870, 1872, 1874.

Murman, Caroline P. "Charles Robinson Story." (Biographical notes) California Historical Society, San Francisco.

Old Burying Ground [opposite First Parish Church]. Newbury, Massachusetts. Headstone.

Rolfe, Mary Adams. Notes from Historical Society of Old Newbury.

Swinscoe, C. Letter to A. N. Bayley, May 7, 1894.

Wawona Hotel Register, 1887–88.

Yosemite Falls Hotel Register, 1877, 1884.

Index

(*Indicates map or illustration)

After many years and several thousand books for numerous publishers, this is the last book to be typeset by Linotype composition by the skilled craftsmen of Holmes Typography, Inc., San Jose, California. Thus, a long-time tradition gives way to the new era of photo-computer composition.